D1271219

The Sayings of Confucius

❖ Wisdom of the East Series ❖

The Sayings of Confucius

*A new translation of the greater part
of the Confucian Analects
with introduction and notes by*

Lionel Giles

Charles E. Tuttle Company, Inc.
Boston • Rutland, Vermont • Tokyo

Published in the United States in 1993 by
Charles E. Tuttle Company, Inc. of
Rutland, Vermont & Tokyo, Japan, with editorial offices
at 77 Central Street, Boston, Massachusetts 02109.

Editorial Note © 1992 Charles E. Tuttle Company, Inc.

Library of Congress Catalog Card Number 93-60007

ISBN 0 8048 1847 9

*This is a facsimile edition of the work originally
published in London by John Murray in 1907.*

PRINTED IN THE UNITED STATES

CONTENTS

EDITORIAL NOTE

WHEN the Wisdom of the East Series first appeared in the early part of this century, it introduced the rich heritage of Eastern thought to Western readers. Spanning time and place from ancient Egypt to Imperial Japan, it carries the words of Buddha, Confucius, Lao Tzu, Muhammad, and other great spiritual leaders. Today, in our time of increased tension between East and West, it is again important to publish these classics of Eastern philosophy, religion, and poetry. In doing so, we hope the Wisdom of the East Series will serve as a bridge of understanding between cultures, and continue to emulate the words of its founding editor, J. L. Cranmer-Byng:

> *[I] desire above all things that these books shall be the ambassadors of good-will between East and West, [and] hope that they will contribute to a fuller knowledge of the great cultural heritage of the East.*

The Sayings of Confucius

INTRODUCTION

CONFUCIUS is one of the few supremely great figures in the world's history. A man's greatness must always be measured, in the first place, by the consensus of opinion in his own country ; the judgment of foreigners can only be allowed to have a secondary value. Especially is this true when the critics are not only foreigners, but belong to a totally different order of civilisation from the men whose greatness they would appraise. For even if they can keep their minds free from purely national bias of the unreasoning sort, they will naturally look for such attributes as are highly prized among themselves, and feel disappointed if these are not much in evidence. They will be apt to see certain defects too plainly, whereas they may easily overlook or fail to appreciate to the full those very qualities on which the title to greatness is mainly based. These errors and prejudices will, doubtless, tend to disappear as more intimate knowledge is gained and the essential unity of human nature shows itself beneath the accidents of custom and environment. But the process will always be slow. The name of Confucius may be deemed sufficiently familiar in the West to render unnecessary any revision of the popular verdict which has already been passed on him. But are his judges equally familiar with the teaching which his name represents ? The name of Shakespeare was well enough known to Frenchmen in the time of Voltaire. Yet how many generations had to pass ere they began to recognise his true greatness ? The parallel between dramatist and social reformer may seem strained, but it is not drawn at random. In both cases, wide differences of language and the inadequacy of translations to bridge the gap, lie at the root of the trouble.

No great man has suffered more than Confucius from the stupidity, the misstatements and the misrepresentations, from the lack of sympathy and generosity, and, in some points, from the pure ignorance of his critics. Early travellers arriving from the West, amongst a people utterly alien to themselves in almost every detail—language, dress, habits, modes of thought, ethical ideals and general view of life—would have done well to walk very warily and, in the Confucian phrase, " to reserve their judgment " on what they saw and heard around them. But patience and discrimination were the very last virtues which these inquisitive newcomers had a mind to practise ; and, unluckily, the extraordinary fame of the national sage marked him out as one of the earliest victims to their thirst for the marvellous. On the strength of Chinese evidence, readily forthcoming and eagerly swallowed, the most exaggerated accounts of this new luminary were poured into the ears of Europe, and it may well be imagined that these enthusiastic reports suffered no diminution in the telling. Confucius was the prince of philosophers, the wisest and most consummate of sages, the loftiest moralist, the most subtle and penetrating intellect that the world had ever seen. He was a statesman, a bard, an historian and an antiquary rolled into one. His sagacity put the most illustrious of ancient and modern philosophers to shame. He was the greatest and noblest representative of the greatest, happiest, and most highly civilised people on the face of the earth. Such extravagant eulogy could only pave the way for disillusionment. When, after the lapse of a hundred years or so, foreigners had painfully acquired sufficient knowledge of the language to enable them to begin translating, after a fashion, parts of the Classics said to have been composed by this glorious sage, or at least containing the choicest pearls of his wisdom still extant, it is not altogether surprising that the results did not come up to the general expectation. Reaction set in, and it soon became the fashion to

s.c.—i*

decry the once much-lauded philosopher. His sayings, which had been extolled as the very epitome of wisdom, were now voted jejune and commonplace. His teaching was found to be shallow, disjointed, unsatisfying. He was blamed for his materialistic bias, for his rigid formalism, for his poverty of ideas, for his lack of spiritual elevation. Comparisons, much in his disfavour, were drawn between him and the founders of other world-systems of religion and ethics. All this before the circumstances of his career had been studied, before the surface of contemporary Chinese history had been so much as scratched, before the host of native commentators and critics had been consulted, or their existence even become known ; above all, before the very book which contained his authentic sayings had been translated with anything approaching to exactness or understanding, or with a faint realisation of its numerous difficulties and pit-falls.

Such was still the deplorable state of things when Legge set to work on his translation of the Confucian Canon, which when completed many years later, with its exhaustive prolegomena, notes and appendices, formed a truly wonderful monument of research and erudition. With its publication, Chinese scholarship was carried at once to a higher plane, and foreign study of Confucian doctrine began in earnest. The heavy accumulations of ignorance and error were in large part removed, and the figure of the great Teacher began at last to emerge from the " obliterating sands of time." His sayings were no longer read as interesting but desultory fragments of conversation, but studied in relation to the events of his life. From various Chinese sources, the chief of which were the Analects themselves and Ssŭ-ma Ch'ien's biography, Legge managed to compile a good and coherent account of the sage's life, work and wanderings, which was an enormous advance on anything that had been done before, and is not likely, even in the future, to undergo any considerable addition or amendment. There are many minor points which may be disputed, and many long blanks which may never be filled up, but taken as a whole, the chronology and the leading events of the life of Confucius must now be considered as finally settled.

If Legge is on firm ground where hard facts are concerned, it is far otherwise when he comes to draw inferences from these facts, to sum up the salient principles of Confucian ethics, and to pass judgment on the character of Confucius himself. His pronouncements on these points, too hastily accepted as final, need to be carefully re-examined and, as I shall hope to show, largely modified if not totally reversed. His opinion, of course, was based chiefly on his own inter-

pretation of the more important sayings in
the Analects, in translating which he had the
oral help of native scholars, besides the benefit
of voluminous standard commentaries. Thus
equipped for his task, it cannot but appear strange
that he, admittedly a great sinologue, should
have gone so far astray as to miss the very core
and essence of the doctrines to the elucidation
of which he devoted most of his life. The explanation may lie in the fact that he was a Chris-
tian missionary in the first place, and only
secondly a scientific student ; he had come to
teach and convert the heathen, not to be taught
or converted by them. This preconceived idea
acted as a drag on the free use of his understanding, and prevented him from entering
whole-heartedly into his subject. We are told
that the Master himself had " no foregone con-
clusions," but Legge's whole attitude to Confucianism bespoke one comprehensive and fatal
foregone conclusion—the conviction that it must
at every point prove inferior to Christianity. A
certain inelasticity of mind showed itself also
in the way in which he approached the work of
translation. He was too apt to look upon a
Chinese word as something rigid and unchanging
in its content, which might be uniformly rendered
by a single English equivalent. Delicate shades
of meaning he too often ruthlessly ignored. Now
there is a certain number of Chinese terms which

mirror Chinese ideas, but have really no absolute
equivalent in English at all, and must therefore
be translated with the aid of circumlocution, and
in such a way as to suit the context and the general
spirit of the passage. It is in such terms, unfortunately, that the very essence and inner significance of the Confucian teaching are contained.
Obviously, if proper equivalents are not given,
the whole sense of the passages in which they
occur will be lost or violently distorted. Worse
still, the judgments laboriously built up on such
rotten foundations will be hopelessly vitiated.
Here, indeed, we have an object-lesson of the
importance, clearly recognised by Confucius
himself, of " defining terms " and making " words
harmonise with things." Indispensable as such
a process is for any investigation in which language plays a part, it is doubly so when words
have to be transplanted, as it were, from their
native soil to one differing from it in almost
every conceivable quality. Such an operation
can only be successful if carried out with the
utmost delicacy and care, and no amount of
erudition can supply the want of that instinctive
feeling for the right word which is the translator's
choicest gift. The scope of the present work
forbids my entering into details, but some broad
examples of failure in this respect will be noted
later on.

Of the life of Confucius only the barest sketch

can be given here, but stress may be laid on one
or two points which it is important to bear in
mind. Confucius was born at a time when the
feudal system, established several centuries earlier
by the founder of the Chou dynasty, was showing
unmistakable signs of disruption and decay. It
is almost certain that China had been feudally
governed from the very earliest times, but Wu
Wang placed the whole system on a seemingly
firmer basis than ever. He divided his realm into
a large number of vassal states, which he bestowed
upon his own kith and kin who had helped him
to the throne. Thus the Empire really came to
resemble the huge united family which Chinese
political theorists declare it to be, and for a short
time all seems to have worked smoothly. But
as the bonds of kinship grew looser, the central
government gradually lost all effective control
over its unruly children, and the various states
were soon embroiled in perpetual feuds and
struggles among themselves, besides being usually
at loggerheads with the parent dynasty. The
state of things that ensued may be likened
(though on a far larger scale) to several Wars of
the Roses going on at the same time, or better
still, to the turbulence of the later days of the
Holy Roman Empire, when the fealty of its members had become merely nominal. Matters were
further complicated in many of the states by the
upgrowth of large and powerful families which

often attempted either by insidious methods or
by open violence to wrest the supreme authority
into their own hands. Thus in Lu, the com-
paratively small state to which Confucius belonged,
there were three such families, the Chi, the
Mêng, and the Shu ; the heads of these clans,
of whom we hear a good deal in the Analects,
had already, by the time of Confucius, reduced
their lawful prince (or duke, as he is generally
called) to a condition of virtual dependency.
On the other hand, they themselves were sometimes threatened by the lawless behaviour of
their own officers, such as the ambitious chariot-
driver, Yang Huo,[1] who thought nothing of
seizing towns or even the person of his own chief,
in order to hold h'm to ransom. Thus, though
the period of the " Warring States " is not usually
reckoned as beginning until after the death of
Confucius, the date is a purely arbitrary one,
inasmuch as his whole life long disturbances were
rife and military operations well-nigh incessant
throughout the length and breadth of China.
In the midst of the prevailing disorder, Confucius
comported himself with an admirable mixture
of dignity, tact and outspoken courage. Wisely
opposing the dangerous tendency to decentralisa-
tion, and upholding the supreme authority of
the Emperor as against his too powerful vassals,
he heartily disapproved of the illegal usurpations

[1] See p. 121.

of the dukes, the great families and the soldiers
of fortune that preyed one upon the other, and
did not shrink on occasion from expressing his
disgust in unequivocal terms. But knowing the
futility of protests unbacked by force, he kept
himself aloof for the most part, and devoted
himself to a long course of study and teaching,
gathering, it is said, as many as three thousand
disciples around him. This is a palpable ex-
aggeration, but there can be no doubt that he
had become a marked man and gained great
fame as a moralist and teacher many years
before he actually took office. In 501 B.C., at
the age of fifty, he at last made his entry on the
political stage by accepting the governorship of
a small town in Lu. Here he is said to have been
eminently successful in the work of reform, and
he rapidly rose to be the most trusted adviser
of Duke Ting, who on one occasion at least
owed his life to the courage and address of his
minister. But it was not long ere the weak and
fickle character of the ruler, carefully manipu-
lated by rivals to Confucius, brought about a
catastrophe. The neighbouring state of Ch'i,
jealous of the new prosperity of Lu under the
régime of the sage, cunningly sent as a gift to the
prince a band of beautiful women, trained in song
and dance, and a number of magnificent horses,
in order to distract his mind from the serious
cares of state. The plotters had evidently taken

the measure of their victim, for the artifice succeeded, and Confucius felt compelled to resign. Then began the weary years of wandering from state to state, in which we cannot follow him here, except to note a sagacious prophecy uttered by a friendly official on the frontier of Wei. Coming out from an interview with Confucius, he comforted the woebegone disciples by telling them that their Master's divine mission was now only just beginning.[1] It may, indeed, be that the ensuing period of homeless exile, hardships and danger, did more to spread the fame of the great reformer than either the few brilliant years of office or those spent as a teacher in the comparative seclusion of Lu. For one thing, it could not but inspire and fortify his followers to observe that the lofty principles which a sudden accession to power had failed to corrupt, were equally capable of standing the test of adversity. His serene and courageous bearing in many a strange and perilous situation proved that the conception of a "higher type of man" was for him no empty ideal, but the worthy object of practical endeavour. It is sad, however, to reflect that the best years of his life had passed before the call came which resulted in his return. Had it not been so long delayed, he would doubtless have thrown himself once more into the arena of public affairs, and begun rebuilding the fabric

[1] See p. 118.

of good government which had been so rudely
shattered thirteen years before. His patience
would have been equal to the task ; but he was
now an old man, worn out by years of travel,
privation and anxiety, at a time of life when the
physical frame begins to demand a certain
measure of quiet and repose. Hence, though he
may be said to have returned to his native state
with flying colours, he took no further active part
in its administration, but devoted the rest of his
life to literary labours which have added materially to his fame. Such were the collecting and
editing of certain old national ballads known to
us as the Odes, and the penning of the Spring
and Autumn Annals of Lu, which may be regarded
as the first real record of authentic facts, as
opposed to the mere string of speeches and
eulogies which we find in the miscalled Book of
History.

To this closing period, too, are to be referred
most of the sayings given in the present volume.
These, together with the invaluable biography
by Ssŭ-ma Ch'ien, which is largely built upon
them, form the only really reliable source of
information about Confucius and his doctrines.
The Chinese title *Lun Yü* may be rendered
" Conversations " or " Discussions," but neither
is a very apt description of the work, which
contains very little discussion in the ordinary
sense. It consists in fact almost wholly of

detached *obiter dicta*, or replies to questions put
by various disciples on subjects chiefly moral or
personal. These sayings were once supposed to
have been collected and committed to writing
by the immediate disciples of Confucius, but
Legge has shown sufficient reason to believe that
they were transmitted orally at first, and did not
take the form in which we have them until at
least two generations after the Master's death.
Nor must it be imagined that they represent the
ipsissima verba of Confucius. No man could
have made offhand remarks in such a crisp,
concise and epigrammatic style. A translation,
in which brevity has again and again to be
sacrificed to smoothness and lucidity, hardly
allows the European reader to form any idea of
the glittering compactness of these sayings in the
original. So far from having been uttered im-
promptu, they appear to have been repeatedly
ground and polished, and shorn of every redun-
dancy, until they shone like diamonds fresh from
the hands of the cutter. At the same time, as
expressing the essence of what the Master thought
and the substance of what he said, it is with good
reason that they are to be found inscribed on
hundreds of thousands of scrolls and tablets in
every corner of the Empire. These gems, however, are unsorted. As in most Chinese philo-
sophical works, there is very little attempt at
orderly arrangement ; even such a rough classi-

fication as will be found in this volume is absent. This is not necessarily to be regarded as a defect : jewels jumbled in a heap often have a charm which they lack when strung symmetrically into a necklace. The only danger is that unwary readers, looking in vain for a beginning, a middle and an end, may jump to the conclusion that Confucius himself was merely a master of casual apophthegms ; they may very easily miss the connecting principles which serve to bind the Confucian teachings into one rounded system. Even the disciples seem to have been in danger of overlooking the whole in their admiration of the parts. It needed the penetration of Tsêng Tzŭ to tell them that the Master's Way was, after all, simple in its diversity, and might be summed up in two words : duty to oneself and charity to one's neighbour. Unhappily, owing to the misinterpretation of these important words, the beautiful simplicity of the Confucian doctrine has long passed unrecognised.

For what has been, and is perhaps even now, the prevailing conception of Confucius in the West ? Does not the name conjure up in most minds the figure of a highly starched philosopher, dry, formal, pedantic, almost inhuman in the unimpeachable correctness of his personal conduct, rigid and precise in his notions of ceremonial, admirable no doubt in his sentiments, but always more a man of words than of deeds ? He has been constantly accused of laying undue weight on things external, of undervaluing natural impulses of the heart. " Propriety," says Legge, "was a great stumbling-block in the way of Confucius. His morality was the result of the balancings of his intellect, fettered by the decisions of men of old, and not the gushings of a loving heart, responsive to the promptings of Heaven, and in sympathy with erring and feeble humanity." It is high time that an effective protest was made against such an amazing piece of misrepresentation. With bitter truth we may retort that " propriety "—that is, the Chinese word *li* which has been cruelly saddled with this absurd rendering—has indeed been a stumbling-block, but a stumbling-block not so much to Confucius as to Dr. Legge himself. The whole tenor of the Master's teaching cries aloud against such wilful and outrageous distortion. Any one who reads the sayings carefully will soon discover that this accusation is not only libellous but grotesque in its remoteness from the truth. If there is one thing more than another which distinguishes Confucius from the men of his day, it is the supreme importance which he attached to *jên*, the feeling in the heart, as the source of all right conduct, the stress which he laid on the internal as opposed to the external, and even on motives rather than outward acts, except in so far as these might be taken as an index to character.

Over and over again he gave proof of the highest and noblest moral courage in ignoring the narrow rules of conventional morality and etiquette when these conflicted with good feeling and common sense, and setting up in their stead the grand rule of conscience which, by asserting the right of each individual to judge such matters for himself, pushed liberty to a point which was quite beyond the comprehension of his age. So far from being " fettered by the decisions of men of old," it was his hand that valiantly essayed to strike the fetters of bigotry and prejudice from the necks of his countrymen. But whilst declining to be bound by the ideas and the standards of others, he was not blind to the danger of liberty degenerating into license. The new fetters, therefore, that he forged for mankind were those of an iron self-discipline and self-control, unaccompanied, however, by anything in the shape of bodily mortification, a practice which he knew to be at once more showy and less troublesome than the discipline of the mind.

Another charge not infrequently heard is one of a certain repellent coldness of temperament and stiffness of demeanour. The warrant for such a statement is not so readily forthcoming, unless indeed it is to be found in the stiff and repellent style which characterises some translations of his sayings. In the Analects we are told the exact opposite of this. The Master, we road there, was uniformly cheerful in demeanour, and he evidently unbent to quite an unusual extent with his disciples, considering the respect and deference universally shown to age and learning in China. Is it at all conceivable that a man of cold and unlovable temper should have attracted round him hundreds of disciples, with many of whom he was on terms of most intimate intercourse, meeting them not only in the lecture-room, as modern professors meet their classes, but living with them, eating, drinking, sleeping and conversing with them, until all their idiosyncrasies, good or bad, were better known to him than to their own parents? Is it explicable, except on the ground of deep personal affection, that he should have been followed into exile by a faithful band of disciples, not one of whom is known ever to have deserted or turned against him? Is coldness to be predicated of the man who in his old age, for once losing something of his habitual self-control, wept passionately for the death of his dearly loved disciple Yen Hui, and would not be comforted?

But it has been reserved for the latest English translator of the Analects, the Rev. Mr. Jennings, to level some of the worst charges at his head. To begin with, he approvingly quotes, as Legge's final opinion on Confucius, words occurring in the earliest edition of the Chinese Classics to the effect that he is " unable to regard him as a great man," quite heedless of the fact that the following stands in the edition of 1893 (two years before his own translation appeared) : " But I must now leave the sage. I hope I have not done him injustice ; the more I have studied his character and opinions, the more highly have I come to regard him. *He was a very great man,* and his influence has been on the whole a great benefit to the Chinese, while his teachings suggest important lessons to ourselves who profess to belong to the school of Christ." This summing-up, though certainly unexpected in view of much that has gone before, does partly atone for the unjust strictures which Dr. Legge felt it necessary to pass on Confucius at an earlier period, though it may require many years entirely to obliterate their effect. What I wish to emphasise at present, however, is the unfairness of quoting an early and presumably crude and ill-considered opinion in preference to the latest and maturest judgment of an authority who at no time can be said to err on the side of over-partiality for his subject.

But this is not all. For after pointing out, truly enough, that Confucius cannot well be blamed for " giving no impulse to religion," inasmuch as he never pretended to make this his aim, Mr. Jennings goes on to pick some holes on his own account, and incontinently falls into exactly the same error that he had previously rebuked in Dr. Legge. " In his *reserve* about

great and important matters, while professing
to teach men, he is perhaps most to blame,
and in his holding back what was best in the
religion of the ancients." What these great
and important matters were, is not made very
clear, but if, as seems probable, the phrase is
simply another way of referring to " the religion
of the ancients," it can only be repeated that
religion was a subject which he disliked to discuss
and certainly did not profess to teach, as is
plainly indicated in the Analects. And the reason
why he refrained from descanting on such matters
was that, knowing nothing of them himself,
he felt that he would have been guilty of hypocrisy
and fraud had he made a show of instructing
others therein. Would that a like candour distinguished some of our own professed teachers
of religion !

The last accusation against Confucius is the
most reckless of all. " There is," according
to Mr. Jennings, " a certain *selfishness* in his
teaching, which had the effect of making those
who came under his influence soon feel themselves great and self-satisfied." As only the
feeblest of evidence is produced to support this
wild statement, it will not be necessary to consider it at any length, though we may ask in
passing whether Yen Hui, the disciple who
profited most from his Master's teaching and
best exemplified it, is depicted as exhibiting

this alleged self-satisfaction in a peculiarly noticeable degree. For an answer to this question the reader may be referred to Tsêng Tzŭ's remarks on p. 128.

The truth is, though missionaries and other zealots have long attempted to obscure the fact, that the moral teaching of Confucius is absolutely the purest and least open to the charge of selfishness of any in the world. Its principles are neither utilitarian on the one hand nor religious on the other, that is to say, it is not based on the expectation of profit or happiness to be gained either in this world or in the next (though Confucius doubtless believed that well-being would as a general rule accompany virtuous conduct). " Virtue for virtue's sake " is the maxim which, if not enunciated by him in so many words, was evidently the corner-stone of his ethics and the mainspring of his own career. Not that he would have quite understood the modern formula, or that the idea of virtue being practised for anything but its own sake would ever have occurred to his mind. Virtue resting on anything but its own basis would not have seemed to him virtue in the true sense at all, but simply another name for prudence, foresight, or cunning. Yet material advantage, disguised as much as you will, but still material advantage in one form or another, is what impels most men to espouse any particular form of religion. Hence it is nothing less than a standing miracle that Confucianism, which makes no promise of blessings to be enjoyed in this life or the next, should have succeeded without the adjunct of other supernatural elements than that of ancestor-worship. Even this was accepted by Confucius as a harmless prevailing custom rather than enjoined by him as an essential part of his doctrine. Unlike Christianity and Mahometanism, the Way preached by the Chinese sage knows neither the sanction of punishment nor the stimulus of reward in an after-life. Even Buddhism holds out the hope of Nirvana to the pure of heart, and preaches the long torment of successive rebirths to those who fall short of perfect goodness. No great religion is devoid of elevated precepts, or has ever failed to mould numbers of beautiful characters to attest the presence of something good and great within it. But in every case the element of supernaturalism, which is of course inseparable from a religion properly so called, introduces a new motive for men's actions and makes it no longer possible for virtue to be followed purely for its own sake, without thought of a hereafter. Thus, if we assent to Comte's famous law of the Three States, Confucianism really represents a more advanced stage of civilisation than biblical Christianity. Indeed, as Mr. Carey Hall has recently pointed out in an article on the subject, Confucius may be regarded as the true fore-

:unner of Comte in his positivist mode of
thought.

His whole system is based on nothing more
nor less than the knowledge of human nature.
The instincts of man are social and therefore
fundamentally good, while egoism is at bottom
an artificial product and evil. Hence the insist-
ence on altruism which we find in the sayings
of Confucius, the injunction to " act socially,"
to live for others in living for oneself. The
most important word in the Confucian vocabulary
is *jên*, which in the following extracts is translated " virtue " only for want of a better term.
Our English word " virtue " has so many different
shades of meaning and is withal so vague, that in
using it, the idea of altruism is often hardly
present to our mind. But in *jên* the implication
of " social good " emerges much more distinctly.
Its connotation has no doubt extended gradually
until it seems often to be rather a compendium
of all goodness than any one virtue in particular.
But this development only means that the word
is following in the track of the thing itself. For
let a man be but thoroughly imbued with the
altruistic spirit, and he may be termed " good "
without qualification, since all other virtues
tend to flow from unselfishness.

The Confucian theory of man's social obliga-
tions rests first and foremost on the fact that he
forms part of a great social machine—an aggre

gation of units, each of which is called a family. The family, in Chinese eyes, is a microcosm of the Empire, or rather, since the family is chronologically prior to the State, it is the pattern on which the greater organism has moulded itself. The feudal system under which Confucius lived naturally accentuated the likeness. The Emperor had, in theory at least, paternal authority over his feudal princes, who in turn, standing to one another in the relation of elder and younger brothers, were regarded as the fathers of their respective peoples. Now, the way to ensure that a machine as a whole may run smoothly and well, is to see that each part shall fulfil its own function in proper subordination to the rest. How is this result achieved in the family ? Obviously through the controlling will of the father, who has supreme authority over all the other members. But this authority is not by any means the mere brute force of a tyrant. It is based firstly on the natural order of things, whereby the father is clearly intended to be the protector of his children ; and secondly, as a consequence of this, on the love and respect which will normally spring up in the minds of the children for their protector. Such is the genesis of filial piety, which plays so large a part in Chinese ethics. It is quite untrue, however, to say with Mr. Jennings, that no corresponding parental duties are recognised by Confucius, as the following anecdote may serve to show. During the sage's short period of office as Minister of Crime, a father came to him bringing some serious charge against his son. Confucius kept them both in prison for three months, without making any difference in favour of the father, and then let them go. The Minister Chi Huan remonstrated with him for this, and reminded him of his saying, that filial duty was the first thing to be insisted on. " What hinders you now from putting this unfilial son to death as an example to all the people ? " Confucius' reply was, that the father had never taught his son to be filial, and that therefore the guilt really rested with him.

For the harmonious working of a family, then, we need respect for authority on one side, and self-sacrifice on the other. The father's object must be entirely altruistic—the good of his family. Then only will he be doing his duty as a father, just as a son is not doing his duty unless he shows honour and obedience to his parents. The all-important element which makes possible the working of the family machine, the lubricating oil that eases the bearings, is not merely filial piety without any corresponding feeling on the part of the parent, but rather a certain subtle principle of harmony and self-control permeating every member of the family group, which restrains egoistic propensities and promotes the common good. This is the Chinese

term *li*, which in this sense of a quality of the soul
is hardly translatable by any single word or
combination of words, but is certainly not to
be rendered by any such atrocious phrase as
" the rules of propriety." [1]

Now Confucius saw that the same general
principles which govern the family are applicable
also to that greatest of families, the State. Here
we have the Emperor, in whose hands the supreme
authority must lie, exercising functions exactly
analogous to those of the father of a family.
But if his is the supreme authority, his must
also be the supreme responsibility. Veneration
and respect are his due, but only because he
identifies himself with the good of the people.
In public affairs, just as in the home, there must
be that same principle of harmony to regulate
the relations of governor and governed, otherwise
the machine will not work. There must be *li*
here as well, but as it is not possible for the
sovereign to maintain with his subjects the personal intimacy which unites a father and his
sons, it is necessary to fall back upon symbols, and
to give outward and visible expression to the
inward sentiments of loyalty and respect which
should animate the breast of each member of
the nation. These symbols are the rites and
ceremonies of which Confucius was considered
such a past-master. He saw indeed their full

[1] See note on p 60.

importance as symbols, but he also knew that, divorced from the inward feeling, they were meaningless and without value. In this way it is easy to see how the word *li*, as a human attribute, acquired its various shades of meaning, from the harmony in the soul which prompts action in accordance with true natural instincts, down to ordinary politeness and good manners—also an indispensable lubricant in the lesser dealings of life between man and man.

It was in the family again that Confucius found a natural force at work which he thought might be utilised as an immense incentive to virtue. This was the universal human proneness to imitation. Knowing that personal example is the most effective way in which a father can teach his sons what is right, he unhesitatingly attributed the same powerful influence to the personal conduct of the sovereign, and went so far as to declare that if the ruler was personally upright, his subjects would do their duty unbidden ; if he was not upright, they would not obey, whatever his bidding. " The virtue of the prince," he said, " is like unto wind ; that of the people, like unto grass. For it is the nature of grass to bend when the wind blows upon it." It must be admitted that Confucius has in this particular somewhat overshot the mark and formed too sanguine an estimate of the force of example. It would be unfair, however, to base our argument on the analogy of modern democratic states, where the controlling power is split up into several branches, and the conspicuousness of the monarch is much diminished. Not that even the constitutional sovereign of to-day may not wield a very decided influence in morals. But this influence was much greater while the king retained full despotic power, and greatest of all in feudal times, when the successive gradations of rank and the nice arrangement of a hierarchy of officials, each accountable to the one above him, were specially designed to convey and filter it among all classes of the community. Had Confucius been able to find a prince who would have acted consistently on Confucian principles, the results might have been almost as grand as he anticipated. The experiment was tried, we must remember, on a small scale, when Confucius himself became governor of a town in the State of Lu. And although one must be chary of accepting all the extravagant tales which gathered round his brief official career, it seems indisputable that this political theory, unlike many others, proved reasonably successful in actual practice.

Of course the weak point is that every king cannot be a Confucius, and unless some practical method can be devised of electing rulers on the ground of merit alone, it is impossible to ensure that their conduct shall serve as a pattern to their people. " Rotten wood cannot be carved," the Master himself once remarked, and he found bitter confirmation of his saying in Duke Ting of Lu. Nothing could ever have been made out of such utterly weak and worthless material. And he afterwards spent thirteen years of his life in the fruitless search for a sovereign who would correspond even faintly to his ideal. Such unswerving devotion to the abstract cause of right and justice and good government cannot but puzzle those who have been taught to regard Confucius as the very type and embodiment of materialistic wisdom and practical utilitarianism. But in truth, strange though it may sound, he was a great idealist who gained his hold on his countrymen by virtue rather of his noble imaginings and lofty aspirations than of any immediate results or tangible achievements. By the men of his own day he was more often than not considered a charlatan and an impostor. It is remarkable that even the two Taoist recluses and the eccentric Chieh Yü (p. 122) should have condemned him as a visionary and a " crank." Similar was the impression he made on the gate-keeper who asked a disciple if his Master was the man " who was always trying to do what he knew to be impossible." This playful sarcasm is really the best commentary on his career, and one that pays him unintentionally the greatest honour. Though often disheartened

by the long and bitter struggle against adverse
circumstance and the powers of evil, he never
gave over in disgust. Therein lay his greatness.
" Wer immer strebend sich bemüht, Den können
wir erlösen," sing the angels in *Faust*, and no
man ever toiled for the good of his fellow-crea
tures with greater perseverance or with less
apparent prospect of success. In this, the truest
sense, he could say that his whole life had been
a prayer (p. 87). He succeeded in that he
seemed to fail. He never achieved the Utopian
object of reforming all mankind by means of a
wise and good sovereign. On the contrary, after
his death confusion grew worse confounded, and
the din of arms rose to a pitch from which it did
not subside until after the momentous revolution
which swept away the Chou dynasty and established a new order of things in China. In a
radically individualistic and liberty-loving country
like China, the feudal system was bound sooner
or later to perish, even as it perished in a later
day among ourselves. But throughout the
anarchy of that terrible period, the light kindled
by Confucius burned steadily and prepared men's
minds for better things. His ideal of government was not forgotten, his sayings were trea-
sured like gold in the minds of the people. Above
all, his own example shone like a glorious beacon,
darting its rays through the night of misery and
oppression and civil strife which in his lifetime

he had striven so earnestly to remove. And so it came about that his belief in the political value of personal goodness was in some sort justified after all ; for the great and inspiriting pattern which he sought in vain among the princes of his time was to be afforded in the end by no other than himself—the " throneless king," who is for ever enshrined in the hearts of his countrymen. It is absurd, then, to speak of his life as a failure. Measured by results—the almost incalculably great and far-reaching consequences which followed tardily but irresistibly after he was gone— his life was one of the most successful ever lived by man. Three others, and only three, are comparable to it in world-wide influence : Gautama's self-sacrificing sojourn among men, the stormy career of the Arab Prophet, and the " sinless years " which found their close on Golgotha.

LIST OF THE PRINCIPAL DISCIPLES

The proper names occurring in the Analects present some difficulty to the European reader, as one and the same person is often referred to in several different ways—by his surname and personal name, by his "style," or by a combination of the two, while among intimates the personal name only is employed. Mr. Ku has on this account eliminated almost all proper names from his translation, using a periphrasis instead. But by this method one misses much of the characterisation which is such an attractive feature of the Analects. I have judged it better to give the names of the principal disciples exactly as they appear in the Chinese, and to provide a table of their various appellations for easy reference. An asterisk denotes the name most frequently used.

SURNAME AND PERSONAL NAME.	STYLE.	MIXED APPELLATION.
Yen Hui	Tzǔ Yüan	Yen Yüan.*
Min Sun } (Min Tzǔ) }	Tzǔ Ch'ien	Min Tzǔ-ch'ien.*

SURNAME AND PERSONAL NAME.	STYLE.	MIXED APPELLATION.
Jan Kêng	Po Niu*	Jan Po-niu.
Jan Yung	Chung Kung*	
Jan Ch'iu	Tzŭ Yu	Jan Yu.*
Chung Yu	Tzŭ Lu*⎫ Chi Lu ⎭	
Tsai Yü	Tzŭ Wo	Tsai Wo.*
Tuan-mu Tz'ŭ	Tzŭ Kung*	
Yen Yen	Tzŭ Yu*	Yen Yu.
Pu Shang	Tzŭ Hsia*	
Chuan-sun Shih	Tzŭ Chang*	
Tsêng Shên ⎫ (Tsêng Tzŭ*)⎭	Tzŭ Yü	
Fan Hsü	Tzŭ Ch'ih	Fan Ch'ih.*
Ssŭ-ma Kêng	Tzŭ Niu	Ssŭ-ma Niu.*
Kung-hsi Ch'ih	Tzŭ Hua	Kung-hsi Hua.*
Yu Jo ⎫ (Yu Tzŭ*)⎭	Tzŭ Jo	

GOVERNMENT AND PUBLIC AFFAIRS

The Master said : In ruling a country of a thousand chariots there should be scrupulous attention to business, honesty, economy, charity, and employment of the people at the proper season.

A virtuous ruler is like the Pole-star, which keeps its place, while all the other stars do homage to it.

People despotically governed and kept in order by punishments may avoid infraction of the law, but they will lose their moral sense. People virtuously governed and kept in order by the inner law of self-control will retain their moral sense, and moreover become good.

Duke Ai [1] asked, saying : What must I do that my people may be contented ?—Confucius replied : Promote the upright and dismiss all evil-doers, and the people will be contented. Pro-

[1] *Ai* was the honorary epithet of the Duke of Lu who was reigning during the last years of Confucius' life.

mote the evil-doers and dismiss the upright, and
the people will be discontented.

Chi K'ang Tzŭ [1] asked by what means he might
cause his people to be respectful and loyal, and
encourage them in the path of virtue. The
Master replied : Conduct yourself towards them
with dignity, and you will earn their respect ; be
a good son and a kind prince, and you will find
them loyal ; promote the deserving and instruct
those who fall short, and they will be encouraged
to follow the path of virtue.

Some one, addressing Confucius, said : Why,
Sir, do you take no part in the government ?—The
Master replied : What does the Book of History
say about filial piety ?—Do your duty as a son
and as a brother, and these qualities will make
themselves felt in the government. This, then,
really amounts to taking part in the government.
Holding office need not be considered essential.

The people can be made to follow a certain
path, but they cannot be made to know the
reason why.

Tzŭ Kung asked for a definition of good government. The Master replied : It consists in pro-
viding enough food to eat, in keeping enough

[1] Chi K'ang Tzŭ succeeded to the headship of the great
Chi family in 491, when Chi Huan died, by whom he was
advised to recall Confucius from his long wanderings. The
sage, however, did not return until eight years later.

soldiers to guard the State, and in winning the confidence of the people.—And if one of these three things had to be sacrificed, which should go first ?—The Master replied : Sacrifice the soldiers.—And if of the two remaining things one had to be sacrificed, which should it be ?—The Master said : Let it be the food. From the beginning, men have always had to die. But without the confidence of the people no government can stand at all.

Ching, Duke of the Ch'i State, questioned Confucius on the art of government. Confucius replied : Let the sovereign do his duty as a sovereign, the subject his duty as a subject, the father his duty as a father, and the son his duty as a son.—A good answer ! said the Duke ; for unless sovereign and subject, father and son do their respective duties, however much grain there may be in the land, I could obtain none to eat.

Tzŭ Chang put a question about the art of governing. The Master said : Devote yourself patiently to the theory, and conscientiously to the practice, of government.

Chi K'ang Tzŭ asked Confucius for advice on the subject of government. Confucius replied : To govern is to keep straight.[1] If you, Sir, lead

[1] The point of the original lies partly in the fact that the Chinese words for " govern " and " straight " are similar in form and identical in sound.

the people straight, which of your subjects will
venture to fall out of line ?

Chi K'ang Tzŭ, being vexed by robbers, asked
Confucius for his advice. Confucius replied,
saying : If you, sir, can check your own cupidity,
there will be no stealing, even though rewards
should be offered for theft.

Chi K'ang Tzŭ questioned Confucius on a
point of government, saying : Ought not I to
cut off the lawless in order to establish law and
order ? What do you think ?—Confucius replied : Sir, what need is there of the death
penalty in your system of government ? If you
showed a sincere desire to be good, your people
would likewise be good. The virtue of the prince
is like unto wind ; that of the people, like unto
grass. For it is the nature of grass to bend when
the wind blows upon it.

Tzŭ Lu asked for a hint on the art of governing.
The Master replied : Take the lead and set the
example of diligent toil.—Asked for a further
hint, he said : Be patient and untiring.

Chung Kung, being Prime Minister to the head
of the Chi clan, asked for advice on governing.
The Master said : Make a point of employing
your subordinates, overlook trifling mistakes,
raise to office worthy and able men.—But,
said Chung Kung, how am I to discover these

worthy men and single them out for promotion ?—
Promote those that you know, was the reply.
As for those that you do not know, will not their
claims be brought before you by others ?

Tzŭ Lu said : The Prince of Wei is waiting,
Sir, for you to take up the reins of government.
Pray what is the first reform you would intro-
duce ?—The Master replied : I would begin by
defining terms and making them exact.[1]—Oh,
indeed ! exclaimed Tzŭ Lu. But how can you
possibly put things straight by such a circuitous
route ?—The Master said : How unmannerly
you are, Yu ! In matters which he does not
understand, the wise man will always reserve
his judgment. If terms are not correctly defined,
words will not harmonise with things. If words

[1] The hidden meaning of this saying is made clear by the
context to be found in Ssŭ-ma Ch'ien's biography of Confucius. The Prince of Wei at this time was the young man
mentioned on p. 128 as holding the throne against his own
father. By so doing he had in some sort inverted the relation-
ship which should have subsisted between them, and each
was in a false position, the father being deprived of his proper
parental dignity, and the son no longer " doing his duty as
a son " (see p. 41). Confucius then is administering a veiled
rebuke to the young ruler, for in saying that the first reform
necessary is the correct definition of names, he implies in
effect that the terms " father " and " son," among others,
should be made to resume their proper significance. An
alternative rendering of *chêng ming* as " rectification of the
written character," though backed by the great authority
of M. Chavannes, can only be described as feeble and far-
fetched, and has been ably confuted by Herr Franke in the
T'oung Pao for July, 1906.

do not harmonise with things, public business
will remain undone. If public business remains
undone, order and harmony will not flourish.
If order and harmony do not flourish, law and
justice will not attain their ends. If law and
justice do not attain their ends, the people will
be unable to move hand or foot. The wise man,
therefore, frames his definitions to regulate his
speech, and his speech to regulate his actions.
He is never reckless in his choice of words.

Fan Ch'ih asked to be taught the art of
husbandry. The Master said : Any farmer can
teach you that better than I can. He then
asked to be taught gardening. The Master said :
Any gardener will teach you that better than I
can. Fan Ch'ih having gone out, the Master
said : What a small-minded man is Fan Hsü !
If the ruler is addicted to modesty and self-
control, his people will not permit themselves
to be irreverent. If the ruler loves justice and
duty, his people will not venture to be unruly.
If the ruler loves sincerity and good faith, the
people will not be slow to respond. Such being
his qualities, the people will flock to him from all
quarters, with their babes strapped to their
backs. What need for him to know the art
of husbandry ? [1]

[1] Confucius is of course merely insisting on the principle
of division of labour, and not by any means depreciating the
value of husbandry or other useful arts. It is not the ruler's

The Master said : If the ruler is personally upright, his subjects will do their duty unbidden ; if he is not personally upright, they will not obey, whatever his bidding.

When the Master went to Wei, Jan Yu drove his carriage. The Master said : What an abundant population !—Jan Yu said : Now that the people are so abundant, what is the next thing to be done ?—Enrich them, said Confucius.—And having enriched them, what then ?—Teach them, was the reply.

The Master said : If a country had none but good rulers for a hundred years, crime might be stamped out and the death-penalty abolished. How true this saying is !

If a kingly sovereign were to appear, by the end of one generation natural goodness would prevail.

If a man can reform his own heart, what should hinder him from taking part in government ? But if he cannot reform his own heart, what has he to do with reforming others ?

Duke Ting [1] asked if there was a single sentence

business to make himself proficient in these, because the task of governing and setting an example to the governed will claim all his attention. Compare Plato's disapproval of πολυπραγμοσύνη, and Confucius' remarks on his owe skill in various arts (p. 88).

[1] The weak ruler of the Lu State (510-494 B.C.), who lost the services of Confucius by his infatuation in accepting the

by which a country might be made to flourish.
Confucius answered : No single sentence can be
expected to have such a virtue as this. But
there is the common saying: "To be a good
king is difficult ; to be a good minister is not
easy." He who realises the difficulty of being
a good king—has he not almost succeeded in
making his country prosper by a single sentence ?
—Is there a single sentence, continued the Duke,
by which a country can be ruined ?—Confucius
answered : No such power can reside in any
single sentence. But there is a saying: "I
have no joy in kingly rule, I rejoice only because
none can oppose my will." Now if the king's
will is good, and none opposes it, all may be well ;
but if it is not good, and yet none opposes it,
has he not almost succeeded in ruining his country
be a single sentence ?

The Duke of Shê [1] asked about the conditions
insidious gift of eighty beautiful singing-girls from the Ch'i
State. See Introduction, p. 16.

[1] Shê was a district of the Ch'u State, which Confucius
visited in 488 B.C. The following anecdote, told by T'an
Kung, is a striking illustration of the above saying. Travelling
with his disciples, the Master came across a woman weeping
and wailing beside a grave, and inquired the cause of her
grief. "Alas ! " she replied. "My father-in-law was
killed here by a tiger ; after that, my husband ; and now my
son has perished by the same death."—"But why, then, do
you not go elsewhere ? "—"The government here is not
harsh," answered the woman.—"There ! " cried the Master,
turning to his disciples, "remember that. Bad government
is worse than a tiger."

of good government. The Master said : Government is good when it makes happy those who live under it and attracts those who live far away.

Tzŭ Hsia, when governor of Chü-fu,[1] asked for advice on government. The Master said : Do not try to do things in a hurry. Do not be intent on small gains. What is done quickly is not done thoroughly ; and if small gains are considered, great things remain unaccomplished.

Tzŭ Lu asked about the service due to a prince. The Master said : Use no deceit, but if you oppose him, oppose him openly.

The Master said : If the ruler cherishes the principle of self-control, the people will be docile to his commands.[2]

Shun[3] was one who did nothing, yet governed well. For what, in effect, did he do ? Religiously self-observant, he sat gravely on his throne, and that is all.[4]

[1] A small city in Lu.
[2] Legge translates : " When rulers love to observe the rules of propriety (!), the people respond readily to the calls on them for service." All the other translators seem likewise to have missed the point, which is elsewhere insisted on by Confucius—that no man is fit to govern others who cannot govern himself. On the meaning of *li*, see Introduction, pp. 30 *seqq.*, and note on p. 60.
[3] A legendary Emperor.
[4] This saying might have come straight from the mouth of a Taoist philosopher. Nor is it the only place where Confucius seems to advocate quietism. Cf. p. 108.

In serving your prince, make the actual service your first care, and only put the emolument second.

The head of the Chi clan was on the point of attacking the small principality of Chuan-yü. Jan Yu and Chi Lu came to see Confucius, and said : Our lord is going to have trouble with Chuan-yü.—Confucius said : Is it not you, Ch'iu, who are to blame in this ? The ancient kings long ago made Chuan-yü the centre of the worship of the Eastern Mêng mountain, and moreover it is situated within the territory of Lu. Its ruler has independent priestly functions.[1] What right have you to attack it ?—Jan Yu replied : It is the will of our master ; we, his ministers, have neither of us any wish to act thus.—Ch'iu, said Confucius, Chou Jên [2] had a saying : " If you are capable of displaying energy, hold office ; if not, resign." Of what use is that minister likely to be, who does not sustain his master in the presence of danger, or support him when about to fall ? Besides, what you say is wrong. If a tiger or a wild buffalo escapes from its cage, if a tortoise-shell or jade ornament is smashed in its casket, whose fault is it, pray ?— Jan Yu replied : But Chuan-yü is strongly fortified, and close to our own town of Pi. If we

[1] Literally, " a minister of the altars to the spirits of the land and grain " ; i.e. a direct vassal of the Emperor, and responsible only to him.
[2] An ancient historiographer, of whom very little is known.

do not take it now, it will cause trouble to our
descendants in a later generation.—Confucius
rejoined : Ch'iu, an honest man hates your
hypocrite who will not openly avow his greed, but
tries instead to excuse it. I have heard that the
ruler of a state or of a clan is troubled not by the
smallness of its numbers but by the absence of
even-handed justice ; not by poverty but by
the presence of discontent ; for where there is
justice there will be no poverty ; where there is
harmony there will be no lack in numbers ;
where there is content there will be no revolution.
This being the case then, if outlying communities
resist your authority, cultivate the arts of refinement and goodness in order to attract them ;
and when you have attracted them, make them
happy and contented. Now you two, Yu and
Ch'iu, are aiding and abetting your master ;
here is an outlying community which resists your
authority, and you are unable to attract it.
Partition and collapse are imminent in your own
State, and you are unable to preserve it intact.
And yet you are planning military aggression
within the borders of your country ! Verily I
fear that Chi-sun's [1] troubles will come, not from
Chuan-yü, but from the interior of his own palace.

When the Master came to Wu-ch'êng, he
heard the sound of singing and stringed instru-

---

[1] The head of the Chi clan mentioned above.

ments. He was pleased, but said with a smile :
Is it necessary to take a pole-axe to kill a fowl ?—
Tzŭ Yu replied : Some time ago, Sir, I heard
you say that the study of true principles made
the ruler beneficent and men of the lower class
easy to govern.—My children, said the Master,
Yen is right. What I said was only in jest.[1]

Tzŭ Chang asked Confucius, saying : What are
the essentials of good government ?—The Master
said : Esteem the five excellent, and banish the
four evil things ; then you will become fit to
govern.—Tzŭ Chang asked : What are the five
excellent things ?—The Master replied : The
wise and good ruler is benevolent without expending treasure ; he lays burdens on the people
without causing them to grumble ; he has
desires without being covetous ; he is serene
without being proud ; he is awe-inspiring without
being ferocious.—He is benevolent without expending treasure : what does that mean ?—The
Master replied : He simply follows the course
which naturally brings benefit to the people.[2] Is

[1] *Wu-ch'êng* means "Martial city," so called from its impreg-
nable position. Tzŭ Yu, when appointed governor, had succeeded in weaning the people from their warlike propensities,
and in introducing the milder arts of peace. This is what made
the Master glad, though he could not help being amused at
the application of the loftiest principles to such a tiny community. About ancient Chinese music we know unfortunately
next to nothing, but it seems to have played as important a
part under the Chou dynasty as in Plato's ideal State.

[2] That is to say, the ruler will always keep the welfare

he not thus benevolent without expending
treasure ? In imposing burdens, he chooses the
right time and the right means, and nobody can
grumble. His desire is for goodness, and he
achieves it ; how should he be covetous ? The
wise and good ruler never allows himself to be
negligent, whether he is dealing with many men
or with few, with small matters or with great.
Is this not serenity without pride ? He has his
cap and robe properly adjusted, and throws a
noble dignity into his looks, so that his gravity
inspires onlookers with respect. Is he not thus
awe-inspiring without being ferocious ?—Tzŭ
Chang then asked : What are the four evil
things ?—The Master said : Cruelty :—leaving
the people in their native ignorance, yet punishing
their wrong-doing with death. Oppression :—
requiring the immediate completion of tasks
imposed without previous warning. Ruthless-
ness :—giving vague orders, and then insisting
on punctual fulfilment. Peddling husbandry :—
stinginess in conferring the proper rewards on
deserving men.[1]

of his people in view, but without indulging in indiscriminate
largess. The ever-increasing doles of money and corn with
which the Roman Emperors were obliged to buy the favour of
the populace would thus have fallen under the condemnation
of Confucius.

[1] The " four evil things " really turn out to be reducible
to two, namely (1) Cruelty—covering the first three ; and
(2) Meanness.

INDIVIDUAL VIRTUE

The Master said : Is he not a princely man [1]—
he who is never vexed that others know him not ?

True virtue [2] rarely goes with artful speech
and insinuating looks.

[1] This is the much-discussed *chün tzŭ*, an expression of
which the stereotyped English equivalent is " the superior
man." But in this there is, unhappily, a tinge of blended
superciliousness and irony absolutely foreign to the native
phrase, which in my opinion makes it unsuitable. " Princely
man " is as nearly as possible the literal translation, and
sometimes, as we shall see, it actually means " prince."
But in the majority of cases the connotation of rank or
authority is certainly not explicit, and as a general rendering
I have preferred " the higher type of man," " the nobler
sort of man," or sometimes more simply, " the good man."
Perhaps the nearest approximation in any European language
is to be found in the Greek ὁ καλὸς κἀγαθός, because that
implies high mental and moral qualities combined with all
the outward bearing of a gentleman. Compare also Aristotle's
ὁ σπουδαῖος, who is however rather more abstract and ideal.

[2] *Jên*, the term here translated " virtue," is perhaps the
most important single word in the Analects, and the real
corner-stone of Confucian ethics. Its primary meaning,
in accordance with the etymology, is " humanity " in
the larger sense, i.e. natural goodness of heart as shown in
intercourse with one's fellow-men. Hence it is sometimes
best translated " loving-kindness " or " charity " in the
biblical sense, though in many cases a more convenient, if
vaguer, rendering is " virtue," " moral virtue," or even, as
in Legge, " perfect virtue."

At home, a young man should show the qualities of a son ; abroad, those of a younger brother. He should be circumspect but truthful. He should have charity in his heart for all men, but associate only with the virtuous. After thus regulating his conduct, his surplus energy should be devoted to literary culture.

In the matter of food and lodging, the nobler type of man does not seek mere repletion and comfort. He is earnest in his affairs and cautious in his speech, and frequents virtuous company for his own improvement. He may be called one truly bent on the study of virtue.[1]

Mêng I Tzǔ [2] asked for a definition of filial piety. The Master said : It consists in there being no falling off.[3]—Fan Ch'ih was driving the Master's carriage some time after, when the latter told him, saying : Mêng I Tzǔ asked me about filial

---

[1] Literally, " he may be called a lover of learning." But " learning " in the mouth of Confucius is generally to be understood as study of the rules of right conduct with a view to their practical application. The object of all learning was to enable a man to develop the natural goodness within him, so as to lead a life of virtuous culture. It was not pursued solely for its own sake, nor had it become, as with us, divorced from all ethical significance.

[2] The chief of the house of Mêng, one of the three great families of Lu, and (according to Ssǔ-ma Ch'ien) a disciple of Confucius.

[3] The reply is enigmatical, but it is clear from what follows that this, and not, as Legge translates, " disobedience," is the true meaning.

piety, and I answered that it consisted in there being no falling off.—Fan Ch'ih said: What did you mean?—The Master replied: That parents should be served in the proper spirit while living, buried with the proper rites after death, and worshipped thereafter with the proper sacrifices.

Mêng Wu Po [1] asked for a definition of filial piety. The Master said: There is filial piety when parents are spared all anxiety about their children except when they happen to fall sick. [2]

Tzŭ Yu put a question on the subject of filial piety. The Master said: The filial piety of to-day reduces itself to the mere question of maintenance. Yet this is something in which even our dogs and horses have a share. [3] Without the feeling of reverence, what is there to distinguish the two cases?

[1] The eldest son of Mêng I Tzŭ.

[2] It is astonishing that Chu Hsi should have tried to improve on the old commentators here, and almost equally astonishing that Legge should have followed him, with this result: "The Master said, Parents are anxious lest their children should be sick" (and therefore children should take care of their persons)!

[3] Here again it is almost incredible that Legge should have adopted such a ridiculous interpretation as the following—without the authority, this time, of Chu Hsi: "The filial piety of nowadays means the support of one's parents. But dogs and horses likewise are able to do something in the way of support." The image conjured up by this sentence is grotesque, to say the least.

Tzŭ Hsia also asked about filial piety. The Master said: It can hardly be gauged from mere outward acts.[1] When there is work to be done, to relieve one's elders of the toil; or when there is wine and food, to cause them to partake thereof—is *this* to be reckoned filial piety?

Tzŭ Kung inquired about the higher type of man. The Master replied: The higher type of man is one who acts before he speaks, and professes only what he practises.

The Master said: The higher type of man is catholic in his sympathy and free from party bias; the lower type of man is biassed and unsympathetic.

A man without charity in his heart—what has

[1] Literally, "colour difficult." This famous sentence, a stumbling-block to native and foreigner alike, surely marks the extreme limit to which conciseness can be carried in Chinese. "The difficulty is with the countenance" is the lame translation offered by Legge, and later scholars have mostly followed in his footsteps, even Mr. Ku Hung-ming failing badly for once. Where all have gone astray is in taking the "difficulty" to exist in the mind of the would-be filial son, instead of being that felt by the onlooker who wishes to gauge the genuineness of the quality in others. Only a few months ago, a new and ingenious interpretation was suggested by my father, Professor H. A. Giles, namely: "To define it is difficult"; but after much consideration I am led to prefer the rendering in the text, inasmuch as the word *sê* is quite commonly used to denote the external as opposed to the internal, form as opposed to essence.

[2] The answer of course is—No; outward acts do not constitute filial piety, unless prompted by a genuine duteous feeling in the heart.

he to do with ceremonies ? A man without charity in his heart—what has he to do with music ? [1]

Lin Fang inquired as to the prime essential in ceremonial observances. The Master said : Ah, that is a great question indeed ! In all rites, simplicity is better than extravagance ; in mourning for the dead, heartfelt sorrow is better than punctiliousness.

The Master said : The true gentleman is never contentious. If a spirit of rivalry is anywhere unavoidable, it is at a shooting-match. Yet even here he courteously salutes his opponents before taking up his position, and again when, having lost, he retires to drink the forfeit-cup. So that even when competing he remains a true gentleman.

It is the spirit of charity which makes a locality good to dwell in. He who selects a neighbourhood without regard to this quality cannot be considered wise.

Only he who has the spirit of goodness within him is really able either to love or to hate.

The princely man never for a single instant quits the path of virtue ; in times of storm and stress he remains in it as fast as ever.

[1] A notable utterance, which may be commended to those who have been taught to regard Confucius as a man of ceremonies and outward show.

The nobler sort of man in his progress through the world has neither narrow predilections nor obstinate antipathies. What he follows is the line of duty.

The nobler sort of man is proficient in the knowledge of his duty; the inferior man is proficient only in money-making.

In serving his father and mother, a son may use gentle remonstrance; if he sees that they pay no heed, he should not desist, but merely increase in deference; if his pains are thrown away, he must show no resentment.

While one's parents are alive, one should not travel to a distance; if one must travel, it should be in a fixed direction.[1]

The age of one's parents should always be kept in mind—on the one hand, as a subject for rejoicing; on the other, as a cause for alarm.

The wise man will be slow to speak but quick to act.

Tzŭ Chang asked, saying: The Prime Minister Tzŭ Wên[2] held office three times, but showed no joy; he lost it three times, but testified no concern. When he ceased to be Prime Minister, he was careful to explain the political situation to his successor. What is your opinion of him?—

[1] In order that the parents may know where their son is.
[2] Of the Ch'u State.

The Master said : He was loyal and conscientious.[1]—Had he not the highest degree of moral virtue ?—That I do not know ; how can one judge of his moral virtue ?—Tzŭ Chang continued : When Ts'ui Tzŭ [2] slew the Prince of Ch'i, Ch'ên Wên Tzŭ, though the possessor of ten teams of war-horses, forsook his wealth and turned his back on the country. Having come to another state, he said : " Here they are as bad as our own minister Ts'ui Tzŭ," and departed. And he repeated this proceeding each time that he came to a new state.[3] What is your opinion of him ?—The Master said : He was pure and incorruptible.—Had he not the highest degree of virtue ?—I cannot say ; how is one to judge ?

The Master said : When the solid outweighs the ornamental, we have boorishness ; when the ornamental outweighs the solid, we have superficial smartness. Only from a proper blending of the two will the higher type of man emerge.

[1] The root idea of this word *chung* is loyalty to *oneself*, devotion to principle, or, as Mr. Ku Hung-ming well translates it, conscientiousness. Loyalty or fidelity to the sovereign is only an extended sense. Here the two ideas appear to be blended, but in a famous passage to be noted further on (p. 118) much trouble has resulted from ignoring the first and fundamental meaning.

[2] A high officer in Ch'i, the state adjoining Lu.

[3] The fact that Ch'ên Wên Tzŭ could not reconcile it with his conscience to settle in any of the states which he visited throws a lurid light on the disorder prevailing in the Empire at this period (547 B.C.). Murder and usurpation were evidently the rule rather than the exception.

All men are born good. He who loses his goodness and yet lives is lucky to escape.

Better than one who knows what is right is one who is fond of what is right; and better than one who is fond of what is right is one who delights in what is right.

Fan Ch'ih asked in what wisdom consisted. The Master said : Make righteousness in human affairs your aim, treat all supernatural beings with respect, but keep aloof from them—then you may be called wise. Asked about moral virtue, he replied : The virtuous man thinks of the difficult thing [1] first, and makes material advantage only a secondary consideration. This may be said to constitute moral virtue.

The Master said : The man of knowledge finds pleasure in the sea, the man of virtue finds pleasure in the mountains. [2] For the man of knowledge is restless and the man of virtue is calm. The man of knowledge is happy, and the man of virtue is long-lived.

The higher type of man, having gathered wide objective knowledge from the branches of polite learning, will regulate the whole by the inner

[1] That is to say, the virtuous act, which he will perform for its own sake, regardless of consequences.
[2] Each finds pleasure in that part of Nature which resembles himself.

rule of conduct,[1] and will thus avoid overstepping the limit.

That virtue is perfect which adheres to a constant mean. It has long been rare amongst men.

Tzŭ Kung asked : What would you say of the man who conferred benefits far and wide on the people and was able to be the salvation of all ? Would you pronounce him a man of moral virtue ? —Of moral virtue ? said the Master. Nay, rather, of divine virtue.[2] Even Yao and Shun were still striving to attain this height.

The man of moral virtue, wishing to stand firm himself, will lend firmness unto others; wishing

[1] As may be inferred from its composition, the character *li* originally had sole reference to religious rites, whence however it came to be applied to every sort of ceremonial, including the ordinary rules of politeness, the etiquette of society, the conduct befitting all stations of life, and moreover to the state of mind of which such conduct is the outcome. This state of mind is one of equably adjusted harmony and self-restraint, and it is in this sense of an inward principle of proportion and self-control that the word is frequently used in the Analects. Why such a vile phrase as " the rules of propriety " was ever coined to express this subtle conception, and retained in every context, however inappropriate, must remain an insoluble mystery. Is it surprising that one of the greatest of world-teachers should still be waiting to come into his full heritage, when his sayings are made to suggest nothing so much as the headmistress of a young ladies' seminary ?

[2] It is interesting to observe that Confucius allows a grade of heroic and almost divine virtue even above that which constitutes complete goodness for all practical purposes, just as Aristotle places his θεῖός τις ἀνήρ above the σώφρων.

himself to be illuminated, he will illuminate others. To be able to do to others as we would be done by [1]—this is the true domain of moral virtue.

It has not been my lot to see a divine man ; could I see a princely man, that would satisfy me. It has not been my lot to see a thoroughly virtuous man ; could I see a man possessing honesty of soul, that would satisfy me. Is it possible there should be honesty of soul in one who pretends to have what he has not ; who, when empty, pretends to be overflowing ; who, when in want, pretends to be in affluence ?

The higher type of man is calm and serene ; the inferior man is constantly agitated and worried.

With sincerity and truth unite a desire for self-culture. Lay down your life rather than quit the path of virtue. Enter not the state which is tottering to its fall. Abide not in the state where sedition is rampant. When law obtains in the Empire, let yourself be seen ; when lawlessness reigns, retire into obscurity. In a state governed on right principles, poverty and low station are things to be ashamed of ; in an ill-governed state, riches and rank are things to be ashamed of.

The man of wisdom does not vacillate ; the

[1] It is only fair to mention that the above is not an exact translation of the words in the Chinese text, though I believe their import to be what I have set down. The point is too technical and abstruse to be discussed here.

man of natural goodness does not fret ; the man of valour does not fear.

Yen Yüan inquired as to the meaning of true goodness. The Master said : The subdual of self, and reversion to the natural laws governing conduct—this is true goodness. If a man can for the space of one day subdue his selfishness and revert to natural laws, the whole world will call him good. True goodness springs from a man's own heart. How can it depend on other men ?—Yen Yüan said : Kindly tell me the practical rule to be deduced from this.—The Master replied : Do not use your eyes, your ears, your power of speech or your faculty of movement without obeying the inner law of self-control.[1]—Yen Yüan said : Though I am not quick in thought or act, I will make it my business to carry out this precept.

Chung Kung inquired as to the meaning of true goodness. The Master said : When out of doors, behave as though you were entertaining a distinguished guest ; in ruling the people, behave as though you were officiating at a solemn sacrifice ; what you would not wish done to yourself, do not unto others.[2]   Then in public as in

[1] See note on p. 60.   This is the solemn nonsense dished up by Legge : " Look not at what is contrary to propriety ; listen not to what is contrary to propriety ; speak not what is contrary to propriety ; make no movement which is contrary to propriety."
[2] Confucius here, as in general, suits his reply to the

private life you will excite no ill-will. Chung Kung said : Though I am not quick in thought or act, I will make it my business to carry out this precept

Ssŭ-ma Niu inquired as to the meaning of true goodness. The Master said : The truly good man is slow of speech.[1]—Slowness of speech ! Is this what goodness consists in ?—The Master said : Does not the difficulty of deciding what it is right to *do* necessarily imply slowness to *speak* ?

Ssŭ-ma Niu asked for a definition of the princely man. The Master said : The princely man is one who knows neither grief nor fear.— Absence of grief and fear ! Is this the mark of a princely man ?—The Master said : If on searching his heart he finds no guilt, why should he grieve ? of what should he be afraid ?

Tzŭ Chang asked how to attain exalted virtue. . . . The Master said : Make conscientiousness and truth your guiding principles, and thus pass on to the cultivation of duty to your neighbour This is exalted virtue.

questioner. In answering Yen Yüan, the model disciple, he had gone to the very root of the matter, making it clear that the essence of true goodness has little or nothing to do with externals. To Chung Kung, who was less advanced and doubtless somewhat lacking in grace or dignity of demeanour, he gives more superficial advice, but winds up by enunciating the Golden Rule, which is the best practical manner of manifesting inward goodness of heart.

[1] There seems to be a play on this word which cannot be brought out in translation.

The Master said : The nobler sort of man emphasises the good qualities in others, and does not accentuate the bad. The inferior sort does the reverse.

Tzŭ Chang asked : What must a man do in order to be considered distinguished ?—The Master said : What do you mean by the term " distinguished " ?—Tzŭ Chang replied : I mean one whose fame fills both his own private circle and the State at large.—The Master said : That is notoriety, not distinction. The man of true distinction is simple, honest, and a lover of justice and duty. He weighs men's words, and observes the expression of their faces.[1] He is anxious to put himself below others. Such a one is truly distinguished in his private and his public life. As to the man who is merely much talked about, he puts on an appearance of charity and benevolence, but his actions belie it. He is self-satisfied and has no misgivings. Neither in private nor in public life does he achieve more than notoriety.

Tzŭ Kung asked a question about friendship. The Master said : Be conscientious in speaking to your friend, but tactful in your efforts to guide him aright. If these fail, stop. Do not court a personal rebuff.

[1] This probably means that he will not rely on words alone in judging of character.

The Duke of Shê addressed Confucius, saying : We have an upright man in our country. His father stole a sheep, and the son bore witness against him.—In our country, Confucius replied, uprightness is something different from this. A father hides the guilt of his son, and a son hides the guilt of his father. It is in such conduct that true uprightness is to be found.

Fan Ch'ih asked a question about moral virtue. The Master said : In private life, show self-respect ; in the management of affairs, be attentive and thorough ; in your dealings with others, be honest and conscientious. Never abandon these principles, even among savages.

The Master said : The nobler sort of man is accommodating but not obsequious ; the inferior sort is obsequious but not accommodating.

The nobler sort of man is easy to serve yet difficult to please. Who seeks to please him in wrongful ways will not succeed. In exacting service from others, he takes account of aptitudes and limitations. The baser sort of man is difficult to serve yet easy to please. Who seeks to please him in any wrongful way will assuredly succeed. And he requires absolute perfection in those from whom he exacts service.

The nobler sort of man is dignified but not proud ; the inferior man is proud but not dignified.

s.c.—3

Hsien said : To refrain from self-glorification, to subdue feelings of resentment, to control selfish desire—may this be held to constitute perfect virtue ?—The Master said : These things may certainly be considered hard to achieve, but I am not so sure that they constitute perfect virtue.[1]

The Master said : A man of inward virtue [2] will have virtuous words on his lips, but a man of virtuous words is not always a virtuous man. The man of perfect goodness [2] is sure to possess courage, but the courageous man is not necessarily good.

Can true love be anything but exacting ? How can our sense of duty allow us to abstain from admonition ?

The nobler sort of man tends upwards ; the baser sort tends downwards.

The princely type of man is modest in his speech, but liberal in his performance.

The princely man has three great virtues,

[1] Being too purely negative.
[2] It is almost impossible, here and in other passages, to make any real distinction of meaning between *tê*, the manifestation of eternal principles in the soul of man, and *jên*, natural goodness of heart, though the former, being more universal and abstract, may be said to include the latter, which generally implies a certain relation to one's fellowmen.

which I cannot claim for myself. He is truly benevolent, and is free from care ; he is truly wise, and is free from delusions ; he is truly brave, and is free from fear.—Nay, replied Tzŭ Kung, these virtues are our Master's own.[1]

The Master said : Is not he a sage who neither anticipates deceit nor suspects bad faith in others, yet is prompt to detect them when they appear ?

Some one asked : How do you regard the principle of returning good for evil ?—The Master said : What, then, is to be the return for good ? Rather should you return justice for injustice, and good for good.[2]

Tzŭ Lu asked about the conduct of the princely man.[3] The Master said : He cultivates himself so as to gain in self-respect.—Does he rest content with that ?—He cultivates himself, was the reply, so as to give happiness to others.—And is he content with that ?—He cultivates himself so as to confer peace and prosperity on the whole people.

[1] This is surely the obvious rendering, yet all previous translators have taken the second *tao* in the sense of " to say." Thus Legge has : " Master, that is what you yourself say."

[2] The principle of returning good for evil, which is here apparently represented as a well-known ethical doctrine, was first enunciated, so far as we know, by Lao Tzŭ. Confucius rejects this vain idealism, and advocates the much sounder and more practical basis for society given in the text.

[3] Here *chün tzŭ* seems almost to denote an actual prince, not merely a man with princely qualities.

By self-cultivation to confer peace and prosperity on the whole people !—was not this the object which Yao and Shun still laboured to attain ?

Tzŭ Kung asked for advice on the practice of moral virtue. The Master replied : If an artisan wants to do his work well, he must begin by sharpening his tools. Even so, among the great men of your country, you should serve the wise and good, and make friends of men who have this moral virtue.

The Master said : The higher type of man makes a sense of duty the groundwork of his character, blends with it in action a sense of harmonious proportion, manifests it in a spirit of unselfishness, and perfects it by the addition of sincerity and truth. Then indeed is he a noble character.

The higher type of man seeks all that he wants in himself ; the inferior man seeks all that he wants from others.

The higher type of man is firm but not quarrelsome ; sociable, but not clannish.

The wise man does not esteem a person more highly because of what he says, neither does he undervalue what is said because of the person who says it.

Tzŭ Kung asked, saying : Is there any one

maxim which ought to be acted upon throughout one's whole life ?—The Master replied : Surely the maxim of charity [1] is such :—Do not unto others what you would not they should do unto you.

The nobler sort of man pays special attention to nine points. He is anxious to see clearly, to hear distinctly, to be kindly in his looks, respectful in his demeanour, conscientious in his speech, earnest in his affairs ; when in doubt, he is careful to inquire ; when in anger, he thinks of the consequences ; when offered an opportunity for gain, he thinks only of his duty.

Tzŭ Chang asked Confucius a question about moral virtue. Confucius replied : Moral virtue simply consists in being able, anywhere and everywhere, to exercise five particular qualities. Asked what these were, he said : Self-respect, magnanimity, sincerity, earnestness and benevolence. Show self-respect, and others will re-

[1] Legge translates *shu* "reciprocity," apparently for no other reason than to explain the maxim that follows. But it really stands for something higher than the strictly utilitarian principle of *do ut des*. Both here and in another famous passage (see p. 118) it is almost equivalent to *jên*, goodness of heart, only with the idea of *altruism* more explicitly brought out. It connotes sympathetic consideration for others, and hence the best rendering would seem to be "loving-kindness" or "charity." The concluding maxim is really nothing more nor less than the Golden Rule of Christ, though less familiar to us in its negative form.

spect you ; [1] be magnanimous, and you will win all hearts ; be sincere, and men will trust you ; be earnest, and you will achieve great things ; be benevolent, and you will be fit to impose your will on others.

Tzŭ Lu asked : Does not the princely man [2] value courage ?—The Master said : He puts righteousness first. The man of high station [2] who has courage without righteousness is a menace to the State ; the common man who has courage without righteousness is nothing more than a brigand.

Tzŭ Kung asked : Has the nobler sort of man any hatreds ?—The Master replied : He has. He hates those who publish the faults of others ; he hates men of low condition who vilify those above them ; he hates those whose courage is unaccompanied by self-restraint ; he hates those who are audacious but narrow-minded. And you, Tz'ŭ, he added, have you also your hatreds ? —I hate, replied the disciple, those who think that wisdom consists in prying and meddling ; courage, in showing no compliance ; and honesty, in denouncing other men.

[1] The Chinese have a proverb : " A man must insult himself before others will."

[2] A good example of the fluctuating content of the term *chün tzŭ*, which in the disciple's question implies morality without reference to rank, and in the Master's reply rank and authority without definite moral qualities.

CONFUCIUS' ESTIMATE OF OTHERS

The Master said : I may talk all day to Hui without his putting in a word of criticism or dissent—just as though he were deficient in understanding. But after he has left me, I find, on examining his private conduct, that he knows for all that how to exemplify my teaching. No ! Hui is not deficient in understanding.

Tzŭ Kung asked, saying : What, Sir, is your opinion of me ?—I would liken you, Tz'ŭ, replied the Master, to a vessel limited in its function.— What sort of vessel ? asked Tzŭ Kung.—A richly ornamented sacrificial vessel, was the reply.[1]

Some one remarked that Yung had goodness of heart but no cleverness of speech.—The Master said : Of what use is cleverness of speech ?   Those

[1] It is said elsewhere in the Analects (see p. 94) that " the higher type of man is unlike a vessel designed for some special use," which means that his moral capacity is not narrow and limited.   Tzŭ Kung, then, it seems, had not fully grasped the higher principles of morality, was wanting in breadth of mind and the larger outlook on life.   His aptitudes, however, were excellent so far as they went, and the Master compliments him here on his proficiency in things relating to religious ceremonial.

who are always ready to assail others with their
tongue are sure to make themselves disliked.
As to Yung's goodness of heart I have no certain
knowledge ; but how would he benefit by having
cleverness of speech ?

The Master said : My teaching makes no head-
way.   How and if I were to board a raft and float
away over the sea ?   My friend Yu would come
with me, I feel sure.—Tzŭ Lu, hearing this, was
glad.   The Master continued : Yu surpasses me
in his love of daring, but he lacks discretion and
judgment.

Mêng Wu Po asked whether Tzŭ Lu had true
moral virtue.   The Master replied : I do not
know.—Asked a second time, the Master said :
Yu might be trusted to organise the military
levies of a large and powerful State, but whether
he is possessed of true virtue I cannot say.—And
what is your opinion with regard to Ch'iu ?—The
Master said : Ch'iu might be entrusted with the
government of a district numbering a thousand
households or a hundred war-chariots, but
whether he has true virtue I cannot say.—And
Ch'ih, what of him ?—The Master said : Ch'ih
might be employed to stand in his official dress at
a royal levée and converse with the visitors and
guests ; whether he has true virtue I cannot say.[1]

[1] Confucius probably wished to impress upon his questioner
that true moral virtue (*jên*) was deeply implanted in the soul,

The Master addressing Tzŭ Kung said : Which of the two is the better man, you or Hui ?—Tzŭ Kung replied : How can I venture to compare myself with Hui ? Hui hears one point and promptly masters the whole. I hear one point and am only able to feel my way to a second.— The Master agreed : No, you are not equal to Hui ; neither of us two [1] is equal to Hui.

Tsai Yü used to sleep during the day. The Master said : Rotten wood cannot be carved, walls made of dirt and mud cannot be plastered : —what is the good of reprimanding Yü ? At first, he continued, my way of dealing with others was to listen to their words and to take their actions upon trust. Now, my way is to listen to what they say and then to watch what they do. This change in me is owing to Yü.

The Master said : I have never yet met a really strong character.—Some one suggested Shên Ch'êng.—The Master said : Ch'êng is a slave to his passions. How can he possess strength of character ?

Tzŭ Kung said : I am anxious to avoid doing

and not to be gauged offhand from the presence or absence of certain superficial signs.

[1] It is passing strange that the clumsy " I grant you " for *wu yü ju* (I and you) should have found favour with translators. Wade even goes one better, by translating : " I award you this praise, Hui does not equal you " !

to others that which I would not have them do to me. The Master said : Tz'ŭ, you have not got as far as that.

The Master said of Tzŭ Ch'an [1] that he had four of the qualities of the princely man :—in his personal demeanour he was grave, in serving those above him he was attentive, in his care for the people he was kind, in his ordering of the people he was just.

The Master said : Yen P'ing [2] knows the art of associating with his friends : however old the acquaintance may be, he always treats them with the same respect.

Ning Wu Tzŭ's [3] behaviour was wise so long as his country was well governed ; when revolution came, his behaviour was stupid. His wisdom may be equalled by others, but his stupidity is beyond all imitation.

Po I and Shu Ch'i [4] never remembered old

---

[1] Prime Minister of the Chêng State in the sixth century B.C. When he had ruled for three years, so great was the change effected that " doors were not locked at night, and lost articles were not picked up on the highway." Confucius wept when he heard of his death.

[2] Minister in the neighbouring state of Ch'i.

[3] A minister of the Wei State in the seventh century B.C. In the revolution referred to the prince was driven from his throne, but afterwards reinstated through the " stupidity," that is to say, the unwavering loyalty and devotion of Ning.

[4] These were brothers, celebrated for their protest against

injuries, and therefore their enemies were
few.

Who will say that Wei-shêng Kao [1] was an
upright man ? When asked by somebody for some
vinegar, he went and begged it of a neighbour,
and gave this to the man who had asked him.

For the space of three months together Hui [2]
would not deviate in spirit from the path of perfect
virtue. My other disciples may attain this height
once in a day or in a month, but that is all.

Po Niu [3] lying sick unto death, the Master went
to visit him. He clasped his hand through the
window and said : He is dying. Such is fate.
Alas ! that such a man should have such an
illness, that such a man should have such an illness !

the overthrow of the Yin dynasty. Rather than live under
the rule of the new sovereign, the great and virtuous Wu
Wang, they wandered away into the mountains to perish
of cold and hunger. This fidelity to the cause of Chou Hsin,
one of the bloodiest and most infamous tyrants in history,
seems a shade more quixotic than the conduct of those who
espoused for so long the fallen fortunes of the house of Stuart.

[1] This was a young man who, if legend may be trusted,
died more heroically than he lived. He agreed to meet a
girl under a bridge, but, woman-like, she failed to keep her
appointment. Though the water was rising rapidly, her
lover waited on, unwilling to quit his post, and finally clung
to a pillar until he was drowned.

[2] This is the man whom Confucius, according to Wade
(see p. 73), ranked below Tzŭ Kung !

[3] Po Niu is said to have been suffering from leprosy, and
therefore he would not allow visitors to enter his room.

The Master said : Hui was indeed a philosopher ! Other men living as he did, in a miserable alley, with a single dish of food and a single bowl of drink, could not have endured the distress. But Hui was invariably cheerful. He was a philosopher indeed !

Jan Ch'iu said : It is not that I have no joy in my Master's teaching, it is my strength that fails me.—The Master replied : Those whose strength fails them fall fainting by the way. What you do is to set up bounds which you will not attempt to pass.

The Master said : Mêng Chih-fan is no braggart. Once after a defeat, when he was bringing up the rear, he whipped his horse as he was about to enter the city gate, and cried : It is not courage that makes me last, it is my horse that won't gallop fast enough.[1]

The Master addressing Yen Yüan said : It is only you and I who would be content to accept

[1] Few will see anything harmful in this anecdote as told by Confucius. Yet it is actually made to figure in the general charge of insincerity and untruthfulness brought against him by Legge. " The action was gallant," he says, " but the apology for it was weak and unnecessary. And yet Confucius saw nothing in the whole but matter for praise." In the first place, Legge entirely ignores the possibility that Mêng Chih-fan was really speaking the truth. But even if it were otherwise, Confucius' only comment is that he was " no braggart." Surely it is an overstrained morality that could be offended by this.

public employment when it was offered to us, and to retire into obscurity when we were dismissed.—Tzŭ Lu then said : If you, Sir, had the conduct of three legions, whom would you associate with yourself in the command ?—I would not, replied the Master, choose a man who would attack a tiger unarmed, cross a river without a boat, or sacrifice his life without a moment's regret. Rather should it be one who would not embark on an enterprise without anxiety, and who was accustomed to lay his plans well before putting them into execution.[1]

The Master said : T'ai Po may be said to have reached the summit of virtue. Having resolutely renounced the Imperial throne, he put it out of the people's power to glorify his act of renunciation ![2]

---

[1] Compare Moltke's motto : " Erst wägen, dann wagen." Tzŭ Lu was noted for his reckless bravery. Evidently jealous of the praise bestowed on Yen Yüan, he makes a delightfully artless attempt to secure some recognition for himself, but only draws down a reproof. The Master's relations with this vain, impulsive, good-hearted disciple often remind one of those subsisting between Dr. Johnson and Goldsmith.

[2] T'ai Po was the direct heir to his father's throne, but knowing that the latter wished to be succeeded by his youngest son (the father of the future Wên Wang, the virtual founder of the Chou dynasty), he went into voluntary exile among the barbarous tribes of the south, but kept the motives of his conduct to himself, and thus obtained no credit for his self-sacrifice.

In the Emperor Yü [1] I find no loophole for censure. His own food and drink were plain, but his offerings to the ancestral spirits showed extreme piety. His own garments were poor, but his robes and cap of state were extremely fine. His own dwelling was humble, but he spent all his strength on the construction of public canals and water-courses. I find no loophole for censure in Yü.

After the word had gone forth, Hui was never backward in his deeds.

The Master speaking of Yen Yüan said : Ah, what a loss ! I used to see him ever progressing and never coming to a standstill.

The Master said : Yu, I fancy, is a man who would stand up, dressed in shabby garments quilted with hemp, among people attired in furs of fox and badger, and not be ashamed. " Hating none and courting none, how can he be other than good ? " [2]—As Tzŭ Lu kept constantly humming over this line, the Master said : This rule of conduct is not enough by itself to constitute goodness.

---

[1] The " Great Yü," who in the reign of the Emperor Yao laboured incessantly for eight years to control the disastrous inundations of the Yellow River, himself became Emperor after the death of Yao's successor Shun, and founded the Hsia dynasty (2205–1766 B.C.).

[2] A quotation from the Book of Poetry, a collection of some 300 ancient ballads said to have been selected and arranged by Confucius himself, and hence raised to the dignity of a " classic."

The Master said : None of those who accompanied me on the journey to the states of Ch'ên and Ts'ai come to learn from me now.[1] Distinguished for their virtuous conduct were Yen Yüan, Min Tzŭ-ch'ien, Jan Po-niu and Chung Kung ; for their skill in speaking, Tsai Wo and Tzŭ Kung ; for their administrative powers, Jan Yu and Chi Lu ; for their literary attainments, Tzŭ Yu and Tzŭ Hsia.

Hui does not help me [2]—he takes such delight in everything I say.

What noble piety [3] is that of Min Tzŭ-ch'ien ! Other men speak of him in exactly the same terms as his own parents and his own brethren.

When Yen Yüan died, the Master wept with

[1] This must have been said by Confucius after his return from exile, when many of his followers were dead or in other parts of the Empire. Ch'ên and Ts'ai are particularly mentioned because it was on the road between these two small states that he met with the most perilous adventure of his life, being surrounded by hostile troops and cut off from all supplies for the space of seven days (see p. 115).   It is not quite clear whether the next sentence should not be taken as a note added by the compiler, giving the names of those who were with the Master on this journey.

[2] By criticism or questioning. Cf. p. 71.

[3] On *hsiao*, occurring in another treatise, Mr. Ku Hungming has the following note : " The word in the text does not mean merely a filial son, but has the meaning of the Latin ' pius '—pious in its full sense, reverential to God, dutiful to parents, good, faithful and orderly in all the relations of life."

passionate grief, so that those who were with him said : Master, your sorrow is too passionate.—Is it too passionate ? he replied. Whose death should be a cause for violent grief, if not this man's ?

On one occasion there were standing in attendance on the Master Min Tzŭ, looking gentle and mild ; Tzŭ Lu, looking upright and soldierly ; Jan Yu and Tzŭ Kung, looking frank and affable. The Master was pleased. " A man like Yu," he remarked, " will not come by a natural death." [1]

The Master said : Why is Yu playing his martial music at my door ?—The disciples began to lose their respect for Tzŭ Lu, whereupon the Master said : Yu has ascended the steps of the temple, though he has not yet reached the inner sanctuary.

Tzŭ Kung asked which was the man of greater worth, Shih or Shang. The Master replied : Shih exceeds and Shang falls short.—Then Shih is the better of the two ?—The Master said : To exceed is as bad as to fall short.

[1] " This prediction was verified. When Confucius returned to Lu from Wei, he left Tzŭ Lu and Tzŭ Kao engaged there in official service. Troubles arose. News came to Lu, B.C. 479, that a revolution was in progress in Wei, and when Confucius heard it, he said, ' Ch'ai will come here, but Yu will die.' So it turned out. When Tzŭ Kao saw that matters were desperate he made his escape, but Tzŭ Lu would not forsake the chief who had treated him well. He threw himself into the mêlée and was slain."—LEGGE, *Life of Confucius.*

The head of the Chi clan was already richer than Chou Kung, yet Ch'iu kept levying taxes for him and adding to his wealth.—He is no disciple of mine, said the Master. My children, you may beat the drum and attack him. [1]

The Master said: Hui reaches the verge of perfection, yet he is often in great want. Tz'ŭ does not resign himself to the will of Heaven, yet his worldly goods continue to increase. His judgments, however, frequently hit the mark.

Tzŭ Lu asked if he should at once put the precepts which he heard into practice.—The Master said: There are your father and elder brothers to consult first; why should you be so impatient to act on what you hear?—Jan Yu asked the same question, and the Master said: Yes, act at once according to the instruction that is given to you.—Kung-hsi Hua then said: When Yu asked if he should put the precepts which he heard into practice, you replied, Sir, that he had his father and elder brothers to consult first. When Ch'iu asked the same question, you said:

[1] This was the disciple by whose agency Confucius was finally restored to Lu. But Confucius was the last man to let private considerations stand in the way when public interests were involved and a crying evil had to be redressed. "Beating the drum" has no reference, as Legge thinks, to "the practice of executing criminals in the market-place." It was simply the recognised signal in warfare for advancing to the attack, gongs being used to sound the retreat.

" Act at once according to the instruction that is given to you." Now I am puzzled, and beg for an explanation.—The Master replied : Ch'iu is apt to hang back, therefore I press him on. Yu has eagerness enough for two, therefore I hold him back.

Chi Tzŭ-jan [1] asked if Chung Yu and Jan Ch'iu could be termed great ministers. The Master said : I thought you had something extraordinary to ask about, and now it turns out to be a question about Yu and Ch'iu. What men call a great minister is one who serves his prince according to the principles of truth and virtue, and when that is impossible, resigns. Yu and Ch'iu, however, can only be termed ordinary officials.—Which is as much as to say that they will always obediently follow their master's will ?—The Master replied : They would not follow him so far as to commit parricide or regicide.

The Master said : Yu is the man to settle a long litigation in a few words.

Tzŭ Kung was fond of weighing other men's merits and defects. The Master said : Surely Tz'ŭ must be a very great sage ! Personally, I have no time for this.

[1] A member of the ambitious family which was scheming to get the whole power of the dukedom into its own hands. The two disciples here mentioned had recently been enlisted in its service, and Chi Tzŭ-jan is anxious to find out how far they can be relied upon in case of need. Confucius sees through his nefarious designs.

CONFUCIUS ON HIMSELF

The Master : I will not be grieved that other men do not know me : I will be grieved that I do not know other men.

At fifteen, my mind was bent on learning. At thirty, I stood firm. At forty, I was free from delusions. At fifty, I understood the laws of Providence. At sixty, my ears were attentive to the truth. At seventy, I could follow the promptings of my heart without overstepping the mean.

Tzŭ Kung was for doing away with the customary sacrifice of a sheep on the first day of the month. The Master said : Ah, Tz'ŭ, you grudge the loss of a sheep, but I grudge the loss of a ceremony

The Master said : In any hamlet of a dozen houses you will surely find men as honest and conscientious as myself, though they may not be so devoted to ethical study.

The Master having gone to visit Nan Tzŭ,[1]

[1] The wife of the Duke of Wei, notorious for her intrigues, and even accused of incest. Needless to say, Chinese commentators are at great pains to explain away this incident in the life of the sage.

Tzŭ Lu was displeased. Thereupon Confucius swore a solemn oath, saying : In whatsoever I have sinned, may I be abominable in the sight of God !

The Master said : My function is to indicate rather than to originate. Regarding antiquity as I do with trust and affection, I would venture to compare myself with our ancient patriarch P'êng Tsu.[1]

The unpretentious hiving of wisdom, patient self-cultivation, and untiring instruction of others —to which of these can I make any claim ?

The failure to cultivate virtue, the failure to examine and analyse what I have learnt, the inability to move towards righteousness after being shown the way, the inability to correct my faults—these are the causes of my grief.

Alas ! what a falling-off is here ! Long is it since I dreamt of Chou Kung.[2]

[1] A grandson of the legendary Emperor Chuan Hsü. He is said to have been over 800 years old when he disappeared into the west in the eleventh century B.C. The last words in the text are taken by some to mean " our patriarchs Lao Tzŭ and P'êng Tsu "—Lao Tzŭ being the founder of Taoism, who is also, by the way, alleged to have disappeared at an advanced age into the west.

[2] One of the most revered names in Chinese history. The younger brother of Wu Wang, he helped materially by his wise counsels to establish the dynasty of Chou. He drew up a legal code, purified the morals of the people, and devoted

There is no one, from the man who brings me dried meat as payment upwards, to whom I have refused my instruction.

I do not expound my teaching to any who are not eager to learn ; I do not help out any one who is not anxious to explain himself ; if, after being shown one corner of a subject, a man cannot go on to discover the other three, I do not repeat the lesson.

If the pursuit of riches were a commendable pursuit, I would join in it, even if I had to become a chariot-driver for the purpose. But seeing that it is not a commendable pursuit, I engage in those which are more to my taste.[1]

The Duke of Shê questioned Tzŭ Lu about Confucius. Tzŭ Lu made no reply. The Master said to him afterwards : Why did you not say : " He is a man whose zeal for self-improvement

himself wholly to the welfare of the State. Confucius in the reforming zeal of his younger days had an ardent desire to see the principles and institutions of Chou Kung brought into general practice.

[1] Legge and others (including even Mr. Ku Hung-ming) make the sense out to be : " If there were any prospect of my being *successful* in the search for riches, I would not hesitate to pursue them by any means in my power." Thus translated, the Master's saying is grotesquely at variance with the whole trend of his conduct and the essential spirit of his teaching. Curiously enough, too, there is nothing in the Chinese itself, so far as I can see, to justify such a startling interpretation.

is such that he forgets to eat; whose happiness in this pursuit is so great that he forgets his troubles and does not perceive old age stealing upon him " ?

The Master said : In me, knowledge is not innate. I am but one who loves antiquity and is earnest in the study of it.

If I am walking with two other men, each of them will serve as my teacher. I will pick out the good points of the one and imitate them, and the bad points of the other and correct them in myself.

My disciples, do you think that I have any secrets ? I have no secrets from you. It is my way to do nothing without communicating it to you, my disciples.

There are men, I daresay, who act rightly without knowing the reason why, but I am not one of them. Having heard much, I sift out the good and practise it ; having seen much, I retain it in my memory. This is the second order of wisdom.[1]

[1] That is to say, the wisest men are those who act intuitively, without having to find their way by any conscious mental process. Confucius disclaims any such intuitive perception of right and wrong in his own case, and confesses that he is obliged to rely largely on objective experience, as acted upon by the critical and receptive powers of his mind. The saying has a distinctly Taoist flavour.

In literary accomplishments I am perhaps equal to other men ; but I have not yet succeeded in exhibiting the conduct of the princely man in my own person.

To divine wisdom and perfect virtue I can lay no claim. All that can be said of me is that I never falter in the course which I pursue and am unwearying in my instruction of others— this and nothing more.—Kung-hsi Hua said : But those are just the qualities that we, your disciples, are unable to acquire.

The Master being grievously sick, Tzŭ Lu proposed the offering up of a prayer.—Is there a precedent for this ? asked the Master.—Tzŭ Lu replied : There is. In the Eulogies [1] it is written : " We pray unto you, O spirits of Heaven and Earth."—The Master said : My prayers began long ago. [2]

The Master was passing through a by-street when a man of the district shouted : Great is Confucius the philosopher ! Yet for all his wide

[1] It is not known exactly what these were—a collection of prayers, a book of rituals for the dead, or panegyrics on the departed.

[2] Confucius speaks of prayer in the sense made familiar to us by Coleridge's line : " He prayeth best who loveth best." In this higher sense his whole life had been one long prayer, and he refuses any mediation between himself and God. Could antagonism to the ritualistic spirit be carried much farther than this ?

learning, he has nothing which can bring him fame.—On hearing this, the Master turned to his disciples and said : What shall I take up ? Shall I take up charioteering or shall I take up archery ? I will take up charioteering !

The Master said : The ancient rites prescribe linen as the material for a ceremonial cap, but nowadays silk is used as being more economical. In this matter I fall in with the general custom. According to the ancient rites, the Prince is to be saluted from below the daïs, but nowadays the salutation takes place above. This is presumptuous, and therefore, though infringing thereby the general custom, I adopt the humbler position.[1]

A high officer asked Tzǔ Kung, saying : Surely your Master is a divine Prophet ? What a variety of accomplishments he seems to possess !—Tzǔ Kung replied : Truly he must be a Prophet, so richly has he been endowed by God. And he has also perfected himself in various arts.—The Master, being told of this, said : Does His Ex-

[1] This saying well illustrates the Master's attitude in regard to ceremonies. He was no stickler for mere outward conformity to rule, so long as the inner meaning of the ceremony was not affected. Now the salutation of the Prince was simply intended to be a way of expressing heartfelt loyalty and respect, and it was only because the new position seemed less respectful that Confucius opposed the change.

cellency really know me now for what I am ?
Being of low condition as a boy, I did become
skilled in various arts—but these are base accomplishments after all. If asked whether the
higher type of man has many such accomplishments, I should say, Not many.[1]

The Master said : Am I possessed of true
knowledge ? Not so. But if an ignorant fellow
from the lower class comes to me with a question,
I will discuss the subject from end to end, and set
it fully before him.

Tzŭ Kung said to Confucius : If you had a
lovely jewel, would you hide it away in a casket,
or would you try to sell it for a good price ?—
The Master replied : Oh, certainly I would sell it,
but I would wait until a price was offered.[2]

The Master said : Out of doors, to tender
faithful service to prince and ministers ; at
home, to be duteous towards father and elder
brothers ; to observe the rites of mourning with

[1] See note on p. 44.
[2] Question and answer are of course parabolical. The
enthusiastic young disciple thinks that his Master, in taking
no steps to obtain official employment, is guilty of " hiding
his jewel in a casket," or, as we should say, " his light under
a bushel." Confucius, however, had a great sense of the
responsibility of office, and was loth to thrust himself forward
uninvited. His chance came at last after fifteen years of
waiting, when Duke Ting appointed him governor of the
town of Chung-tu.

the utmost care ; to avoid being overcome with wine :—which of these virtues have I ?

In matters pertaining to ceremonies and music, the ancients were more or less uncivilised in comparison with the refinement of a later age. Nevertheless, in practice I take the earlier period as my guide.[1]

As an arbiter in litigation I am no better than other men. But surely the grand object to achieve is that there shall be no litigation at all.[2]

Wei-shêng Mou,[3] addressing Confucius, said : Ch'iu, why is it you keep hopping about thus from place to place ? Is it not in order to show off your fine rhetoric ?—Confucius replied : I do not allow myself to indulge in fine rhetoric ; no, it is because I consider obstinacy a fault.[4]

The Master said : There are none who know

[1] Another proof, if one were needed, that Confucius' instincts were all for simplicity and not elaboration in ceremonies.

[2] Said by Confucius when he was Minister of Justice in Lu.

[3] Evidently an older man, from his use of the personal name, not to speak of his disrespectful tone.

[4] Confucius, like other great men, was not exempt from the usual fate of seeing his actions derided and his motives misunderstood. Here we have a gibe thrown at his wandering from state to state, for the purpose, it is insinuated, of making a living by his wits. The answer is, that to have remained in Lu or any other state where he was plainly not wanted, would have been merely stupid persistency.

me for what I am.—Tzŭ Kung said : How is it,
Sir, that none know you ?—The Master replied :
I make no complaint against Heaven, neither do
I blame my fellow-men. In the study of virtue
I begin at the bottom and tend upwards.[1]
Surely Heaven knows me for what I am.

Tz'ŭ, do you look upon me as a man who has
studied and retained a mass of various knowledge ?
—I do, he replied. Am I wrong ?—You are
wrong, said the Master. All my knowledge is
strung on one connecting thread.[2]

I used to spend whole days without food and
whole nights without sleep, in order to meditate.

[1] This accounts for men taking no notice of him. Most
so-called sages start with grandiose ideals and high-flown
utterances, in order to attract attention.

[2] This is rightly considered to be one of the most important
of the Master's sayings, because it gives the clue to his whole
philosophy and view of life. The "connecting thread,"
as we learn from another passage (see p. 118), is simply the
moral life, which consists in being true to oneself and good to
one's neighbour. Confucius wished to impress upon his
disciple that he was no mere amasser of knowledge nor lover
of learning for learning's sake. The one thing necessary,
in his eyes, was to be able to lead, in the highest sense of the
word, a moral life, and this was the real object of all learning,
the end and aim of all knowledge. Throughout the Analects,
as we have already seen, the usual word for "learning" always
means or implies the study of virtue, the striving after self-
improvement. Like Socrates, Confucius was purely a *moral*
philosopher, and would certainly have rejected the sharp
distinction we draw nowadays between mental and moral
science.

But I made no progress. Study, I found, was better.

Pi Hsi [1] sent an invitation to Confucius, and the Master wished to go. Tzŭ Lu, however, said : Once upon a time, Sir, I heard you say that the nobler sort of man would not enter into intimacy with one who laid himself out to do wrong. Now Pi Hsi has raised the standard of rebellion in Chung-mou. How can you think of going thither ?—True, replied the Master. Those were my words. But is there not a saying : " The hard may be rubbed without losing its substance ; the white may be steeped without losing its purity " ? Am I then a bitter gourd—fit only to be hung up and not eaten ?

[1] A rebellious official in the Chin State. On more than one occasion in his career, Confucius made it plain that he declined to be bound by narrow convention or hampered by the fear of what people might say of him. To keep clear of bad associates was no doubt an excellent principle, but Confucius may have seen some justification for Pi Hsi's course of action, and in any case he was no longer of an age to be easily corrupted by evil communications. Knowing that rules were never meant to be so rigid as to admit of no exceptions, he felt it his primary duty to go where he could do good. Cf. the visit to Nan Tzŭ (p. 83), the mere idea of which would have horrified an ordinary teacher of morality.

MISCELLANEOUS SAYINGS

The Master said : To learn, and to practise on occasion what one has learnt—is this not true pleasure ? The coming of a friend from a far-off land—is this not true joy ?

Make conscientiousness and sincerity your grand object. Have no friends not equal to yourself. If you have done wrong, be not ashamed to make amends.

Observe the bent of a man's will when his father is alive, and his actions after his father is dead. If during the three years of mourning he does not swerve from his father's principles, he may be pronounced a truly filial son.

The Odes [1] are three hundred in number, but their purport may be summed up in a word :— Have no depraved thoughts.

[1] The rather inappropriate name given by foreigners to the songs or ballads contained in the *Shih Ching* or Book of Poetry (see note on p. 78). Confucius is said to have selected these three hundred odd pieces from a much larger pre-existing mass of material, but his language here hardly strikes us as that likely to be used by a man speaking of his own compilation.

Observe a man's actions; scrutinise his motives; take note of the things that give him pleasure. How then can he hide from you what he really is ?

Acquire new knowledge whilst thinking over the old, and you may become a teacher of others.

The higher type of man is not like a vessel which is designed for some special use.[1]

Study without thought is vain ; thought without study is perilous.

Absorption in the study of the supernatural is most harmful.

Yu, shall I tell you what true knowledge is ? When you know, to know that you know, and when you do not know, to know that you do not know—that is true knowledge.

Tzŭ Chang was studying with a view to official preferment. The Master said to him : Among the various things you hear said, reserve your judgment on those which seem doubtful, and give cautious utterance to the rest : then you will seldom fall into error. Among the various things you see done, set aside those which seem dangerous, and cautiously put the others into

[1] That is to say, he is not limited in his functions like a vessel or implement, not " borné " or a man of one idea. Cf. note on p. 71.

practice : then you will seldom have occasion for repentance. If you seldom err in your speech, and seldom have to repent of your actions, official preferment will come of itself.

The Master said : I do not see how a man without sincerity can be good for anything. How can a cart or carriage be made to go without yoke or cross-bar ?

To sacrifice to a spirit with which you have nothing to do, is mere servility.

To shirk your duty when you see it before you, shows want of moral courage.

Some one inquired as to the meaning of the Great Sacrifice. The Master said : I do not know. He who knew its meaning would find it as easy to govern the Empire as to look upon this (pointing to his palm).[1]

Wang-sun Chia [2] asked, saying : What means the adage, " Better be civil to the kitchen-god than to the god of the inner sanctum " ?—The

[1] Every ceremonial rite being symbolical of some portion of the world's harmony, and the Great Sacrifice being the head and fount as it were of all the rest, it follows that the man who could penetrate its profound symbolism would have the whole system of morals and government unrolled before his eyes.

[2] Prime Minister of the Wei State, who suspected Confucius of coming to seek office, and took this means of hinting that the real power lay with himself and not with the Duke.

Master replied : The adage is false.   He who sins against Heaven can rely on the intercession of none.

The Master said : He who serves his prince with all the proper ceremony will be accounted by men a flatterer.

It is bootless to discuss accomplished facts, to protest against things past remedy, to find fault with things bygone.

How am I to regard one who has rank without liberality, who performs ceremonies without reverence, who approaches the rites of mourning without sorrow ?

Men's faults are characteristic.[1] It is by observing a man's faults that one may come to know his virtues.

Having heard the True Way in the morning, what matters it if one should come to die at night ?

The scholar who is bent on studying the principles of virtue, yet is ashamed of bad clothes and coarse food, is not yet fit to receive instruction.

Instead of being concerned that you have no office, be concerned to think how you may fit yourself for office. Instead of being concerned that you are not known, seek to be worthy of being known.

[1] After some hesitation, I have adopted this clever rendering of Mr. Ku Hung-ming, as being the only one that fits well with the next sentence.

When you see a good man, think of emulating him ; when you see a bad man, examine your own heart.

The ancients hesitated to give their thoughts utterance : they were afraid that their actions might not be equal to their words.

Few are those who err on the side of self-restraint.[1]

Virtue cannot live in solitude : neighbours are sure to grow up around it.[2]

Chi Wên Tzŭ[3] used to reflect thrice before he acted. When told of this, the Master said : Twice would do.

The Master said : Alas ! I have never met a man who could see his own faults and arraign himself at the bar of his own conscience.

Tzŭ Hua having been sent on a mission to the Ch'i State, Jan Ch'iu begged for a gift of grain for his mother. The Master said : Give her a peck.—The disciple asking for more, he said :

[1] A few other renderings of this sentence will illustrate at once the elasticity of the Chinese language, and the difficulty of making it flow into European moulds.—LEGGE : " The cautious seldom err." WADE : " It seldom happens that a man errs through excess of moderation." JENNINGS : " Those who keep within restraints are seldom losers." KU HUNG-MING : " He who wants little seldom goes wrong."

[2] I.e. virtue begets virtue.

[3] A member of the great Chi family, who held office in Lu.

s.c.—4

Give her then a bushel.—But Jan Ch'iu eventually gave her as much as five hundredweight of grain. Then the Master rebuked him, saying : When Ch'ih went to the Ch'i State, he was conveyed by a team of sleek horses and was wearing costly fur garments. Now I have heard that the princely man succours the distressed, but will not add to the opulence of the wealthy.

Yüan Ssŭ, having been made governor of a district, was presented with nine hundred measures of grain.[1] He declined them. The Master said : Do not decline them. May they not be distributed among the villages and townships of your neighbourhood ?

The Master said : Who can go out of a house except by the door ? In life, why not pass likewise through the door of virtue ?[2]

You may speak of higher subjects to those who rise above the average level of mankind, but not to those who fall below it.

With coarse food to eat, water to drink, and the bended arm as a pillow, happiness may still exist. Wealth and rank unrighteously obtained seem to me as insubstantial as floating clouds.

The inhabitants of Hu-hsiang were uncon-

[1] The proper allowance for an officer in his station.
[2] As being, in the end, the most natural and least troublesome route to take.

versable people, and when a young man from those parts came to see Confucius, the disciples hesitated to let him in. But the Master said : When a man comes to me, I accept him at his best, not at his worst. Why make so much ado ? When a man washes his hands before paying a visit, and you receive him in that clean state, you do not thereby stand surety for his always having been clean in the past.

The Master said : Is virtue then so remote ? I have only to show a desire for virtue, and lo ! it is here.

The Master said : Prodigality begets arrogance,[1] parsimony begets niggardliness. But it is better to be niggardly than arrogant.

Without due self-restraint,[2] courtesy becomes oppressive, prudence degenerates into timidity, valour into violence, and candour into rudeness.

Love of daring and dread of poverty lead to

[1] It is impossible to find an exact equivalent for this negative expression " non-yieldingness," " non-humility." But the dominant idea is one of *selfishness*, and therefore such renderings as " insubordination " (Legge), " frowardness " (Wade), " excess " (Ku Hung-ming), are rather wide of the mark.

[2] For note on *li*, see p. 60. Here again it is the inner sense of moral proportion and harmony, which prevents any quality from being carried to excess. Not a translator but has come to grief over this word, though Mr. Ku is not so far off with " judgment." That, however, makes of it an intellectual principle rather than what it really is—a moral sense.

sedition. The man without natural virtue, if pursued by the hatred of society, will become a desperado.

If a man is proud and avaricious, though his other qualities may embrace all that was fine in the character of Chou Kung, they are not worth taking into account.

It is not easy to find a man who after three years of self-cultivation [1] has not reached happiness.

He who is out of office should not meddle in the government.

Hot-headedness without honesty; ignorance without ingenuousness; simplicity without sincerity:—such characters I do not understand. [2]

Pursue the study of virtue as though you could never reach your goal, and were afraid of losing the ground already gained.

The Master said: I have not met one whose love of virtue was equal to his love of sensual beauty.

Though in making a mound I should stop when but one more basketful of earth would complete it, the fact remains that I *have* stopped. On the other hand, if in levelling it to the ground I

[1] Literally, " learning." See notes on pp. 53 and 91.
[2] The commentators seem right in their explanation, that a man's defects are usually redeemed by certain corresponding qualities; when even these are absent, the case is hopeless.

advance my work by but one basketful at a time, the fact remains that I *am* advancing.[1]

Alas! there are sprouting crops which never come into ear. There are others which, having come into ear, never ripen into grain.

We ought to have a wholesome respect for our juniors. Who knows but that by-and-by they may prove themselves equal to the men of to-day? It is only when they reach the age of forty or fifty without distinguishing themselves that we need no longer be afraid of them.

Words of just admonition cannot fail to command a ready assent. But practical reformation is the thing that really matters. Words of kindly advice cannot fail to please the listener. But subsequent meditation on them is the thing that really matters. I can make nothing of the man who is pleased with advice but will not meditate on it, who assents to admonition but does not reform.

A great army may be robbed of its leader, but nothing can rob one poor man of his will.

It is only when the cold season comes that we know the pine and cypress to be evergreens.[2]

[1] This is the best I can make of a vexed passage. Legge's translation is poor, but he is right with regard to the lesson intended—" that repeated acquisitions individually small will ultimately amount to much, and that the learner is never to give over."

[2] Men are known in time of adversity.

Let a pupil join with you in self-cultivation before you let him approach the general truths of philosophy, but let him approach these general truths before he is allowed to form his character for good. He should have formed his character for good before he is allowed to make exceptions to a general rule.

When Yen Yüan died, the Master said : Alas ! God has forsaken me, God has forsaken me !

On the death of Yen Yüan, the disciples wanted to give him a sumptuous funeral, but the Master said, Better not.[1] Nevertheless, the disciples did give him a sumptuous funeral, whereupon the Master said : Hui looked upon me as his father, yet I have not been able to treat him as my son. The fault is not in me, but in you, my disciples.

Chi Lu inquired concerning men's duty to spirits. The Master replied : Before we are able to do our duty by the living, how can we do it by the spirits of the dead ?—Chi Lu went on to inquire about death. The Master said :

---

[1] Because the family was very poor and could ill afford to bear the expense. It is not the least of this great man's titles to fame that he resolutely opposed the tide of popular sentiment in this matter, and could see the iniquity of sacrificing the living to the dead, even when the funeral of his dearly beloved disciple was in question. The moral courage of such an attitude in a country like China, where religion is largely connected with the propitiation of spirits, can hardly be cverestimated.

Before we know what life is, how can we know what death is ?

Tzŭ Chang asked a question about clearness of mental vision. The Master said : He whose mind is proof against the slow-soaking poison of slander and the sharp stings of calumny, may be called clear-sighted, and far-seeing as well.

The Master said : A man may know the three hundred odes by heart, but if he proves himself incapable when given a post in the government, or cannot make a speech unaided when sent on a foreign mission, of what use to him is all his learning ?

Tzŭ Kung asked, saying : What may be said of a man who is beloved by all his fellow-townsmen ?—The Master replied : That is not enough to go upon.—What of one who is hated by all his fellow-townsmen ?—The Master replied : Neither is that enough to go upon. It would be otherwise if, among his fellow-townsmen, the good loved him and the wicked hated him.

The Master said : A good man must have trained the people for seven years before they are fit to go to war.

To take an untrained multitude into battle is equivalent to throwing them away.

In a well-governed country, speak boldly and

act boldly. In a country where lawlessness prevails, let your actions be bold but your speech tactful.

It is harder to be poor without murmuring, than to be rich without arrogance.

The men of olden times who studied virtue had only their own improvement in view ; those who study it now have an eye to the applause of others.

Refusal to instruct one who is competent to learn entails the waste of a man. Instruction of one who is incompetent to learn entails waste of words. The wise man is he who wastes neither men nor words.

Those whose care extends not far ahead will find their troubles near at hand.

He who requires much from himself and little from others will be secure from hatred.

If a man is not in the habit of asking, " What do you make of this ? what do you make of that ? " I can make nothing of *him*.

Hopeless indeed is the case of those who can herd together all day long without once letting their conversation reach a higher plane,[1] but are content to bandy smart and shallow wit.

[1] Literally, " reach righteousness."

When a man is generally detested, or when he is generally beloved, closer examination is necessary.[1]

It is the man that is able to develop his virtue, not virtue that develops the man.[2]

The real fault is to have faults and not try to amend them.

Where there is education, there is no distinction of class.

Men who differ in their principles cannot help each other in their plans.

If language is lucid, that is enough.

There are three errors to be avoided in the presence of a great man. The first is precipitancy —speaking before it is your turn to speak ; the second is bashfulness—not speaking when your turn comes ; and the third is heedlessness— speaking without observing the countenance of the listener.

There are three impulses against which the nobler sort of man is on his guard. In the period of youth, when the heyday in the blood has not yet subsided, he guards against lustfulness ; in

[1] Before subscribing to the popular judgment. Cf. saying on p. 103.
[2] I.e. mere passivity, as advocated by the Taoists, will not do.

the prime of life, when the physical frame is vigorous and strong, he guards against pugnacity ; in old age, when the vital forces are in their decline, he guards against the greed of gain.[1]

The highest class of men are they whose knowledge is innate ; next to these are they whose knowledge is acquired by study [2] ; after them come those who are dull-witted, yet strive to learn ; while those who are dull-witted and will make no effort to learn are the lowest of the people.

" When you see the good, act as though you could never quite come up with it ; when you are brought face to face with evil, act as though you were trying the heat of boiling water " :— I have heard some such saying as this, and I have seen men live up to it. " Dwell in retirement, in order to work out your aims ; practise righteousness, in order to apprehend the Truth " :— such a saying I have heard, but I have never seen a man live up to it.[3]

---

[1] These numerical categories are hardly more than a conventional form into which the Chinese are fond of throwing ethical and other teaching. Needless to say, they are not to be considered as exhaustive.

[2] Confucius, as we have seen (p. 86), puts himself in this second class.

[3] The difference lies in the *set purpose* of studying virtue in a systematic way, and not merely doing right when occasion offers.

Men's natures are alike ; it is their habits that carry them far apart.

Only two classes of men never change : the wisest of the wise and the dullest of the dull.

Speaking to Tzǔ Lu, the Master said : Have you ever heard, Yu, of the six shadows which attend six several virtues ?—No, he replied.— Sit down, then, and I will tell you. Love of goodness without the will to learn [1] casts the shadow called foolishness. Love of knowledge without the will to learn casts the shadow called instability. Love of truth without the will to learn casts the shadow called insensibility. Love of candour without the will to learn casts the shadow called rudeness. Love of daring without the will to learn casts the shadow called turbulence. Love of firmness without the will to learn casts the shadow called eccentricity.

Ceremonies, forsooth ! Can ceremonies be reduced to a mere matter of silken robes and jade ornaments ? Music, forsooth ! Can music be reduced to a mere matter of bells and drums ? [2]

[1] " The will to learn " is a necessarily vague rendering of the equally vague original. It means here a desire for moral culture, which is nothing else than the development of that inner sense of harmony and proportion (*li*) referred to on p. 99. Good instincts, according to Confucius, are not enough to produce virtues, unless they are supplemented by careful cultivation of this moral sense.

[2] A magnificent array of vestments and chalices will no

Men who are grave and stern in appearance, but inwardly weak and unprincipled—are they not comparable to the lowest class of humanity— sneaking thieves that break into houses by night ?

Your goody-goody people are the thieves of virtue.

The Master said : Would that I could do without speaking !—Tzŭ Kung said : If our Master never spoke, how could we, his disciples, transmit his doctrines ?—The Master replied : Does God speak ? The four seasons hold on their course, and all things continue to live and grow. Yet, tell me, does God speak ?

Girls and servants are the most difficult people to handle. If you treat them familiarly, they become disrespectful ; if you keep them at a distance, they resent it.

more constitute a true ceremony than a number of musical instruments alone, without the brain of a composer, can produce music. The whole value of a ceremony is determined by the state of mind of the person who performs it.

PERSONALIA

In his moments of leisure, the Master's manner was uniformly cheerful and smiling.

If the Master happened to be dining beside one who was in mourning for his parents, he never ate a full meal. He never sang on any day in the course of which he had been bewailing a death.

The Master would never talk about prodigies, feats of strength, crime, or supernatural beings.[1]

The Master made four things the subject of his teaching : a knowledge of literature and the arts, conduct, conscientiousness and truthfulness.[2]

The Master fished with a line but not with a net. When he went out with bow and arrow, he only shot at birds on the wing.

If the Master happened to be with singers, and they sang a piece well, he would get them to

[1] Under these circumstances, it is easy to imagine how edified he would be by the modern daily press, which subsists almost entirely on these very topics.

[2] I am unable to improve on this rendering, which is borrowed from Mr. Ku Hung-ming.

repeat it, when he would also join in the song himself.

The Master was affable, yet grave ; stern, but not fierce; attentive in his behaviour, and yet calm.

The Master seldom spoke of money-making, of the laws of Providence, or of moral virtue.[1]

There were four words of which the Master barred the use : he would have no " shall's," no " must's," no " certainly's," no " I's." [2]

Whenever the Master saw a person in mourning, or in official robes, or one who was blind, he would at once rise from his seat, even though the other were his junior ; or if he passed them in the street, he would quicken his step.[3]

Once when the Master was lying seriously ill, Tzǔ Lu got the disciples to act the part of Ministers of State.[4] In an interval of his sickness, Con-

---

[1] This statement—at least as regards moral virtue (*jên*)— seems hopelessly at variance with the evidence of the Analects. Perhaps no more is meant than that he was unwilling to dogmatise on such a delicate subject. On p. 72, for instance, he refuses to judge whether certain disciples have true moral virtue or not.

[2] This is Mr. Jennings's interpretation, and it seems to me the simplest and best.

[3] Thus showing, says a commentator, his sympathy with sorrow, his respect for rank, his tenderness for the afflicted. Quickening his pace was also a mark of respect.

[4] Just as though Confucius had his own Court and *entour-age*, nke a feudal prince. This probably happened during his exile in some foreign state, where the chance of his obtain-

fucius said : What a long time Yu has been keeping up this imposture ! In pretending to have ministers attendant on me when I have none, whom am I deceiving ? Am I deceiving God ? But apart from that, is it not better that I should breathe my last in the arms of my disciples, than that I should die in the midst of officials ? And after all, though I may not be accorded the honour of a public funeral, I am not dying out on the high road.

The Master wished to settle among the nine eastern tribes. Some one said : How can you ? They are savages.—The Master replied : If a higher type of man dwelt in their midst, how could their savage condition last ?

Confucius in his native village was simple and unassuming. He gave the impression of being no great speaker. In the ancestral temple and at Court he spoke fluently, but with a certain reserve.

At Court, he spoke to the ministers of lower rank with frankness and affability. To those of higher rank he spoke quietly, but with decision. In the presence of his Sovereign, he seemed full of awe, but at the same time grave and collected.

When employed by the Prince in the reception of distinguished visitors, his expression would

ing a public funeral would doubtless be proportionate to the display made by his followers.

change, and his legs seemed to bend under him. Standing in the presence of the visitors, he saluted them with clasped hands, turning about from right to left, and keeping the skirt of his robe properly adjusted, back and front. He then hastened forward with arms extended like the wings of a bird. When a visitor departed, he would report in that sense to the Prince, saying : " The visitor is not looking back." [1]

When he entered the gate of the palace, he seemed to bend his body as though the gate were not large enough to let him pass. He did not stand in the middle of the doorway, nor in passing through did he set foot on the threshold. When he passed the Prince's throne, his expression seemed to change, his legs seemed to bend under him, and words seemed to fail him. Holding up his robe with both hands, he ascended the daïs, his body slightly bent, and holding his breath as though he dared not breathe. When he came out from his audience and had descended the first step, his countenance lost its anxious expression, and he looked serene and happy. When he reached the bottom of the steps, he hastened away with his arms outstretched like wings ; but when he got back to his place, he still seemed full of awe.

[1] " The ways of China, it appears, were much the same anciently as now. A guest turns round and bows repeatedly in leaving, and the host cannot return to his place till these salutations are ended."—LEGGE.

He carried the Prince's regalia with body slightly bent, as though he could hardly support its weight; he raised it to the height of his head, and lowered it again to the height of his chest. His countenance indicated nervousness, and he dragged his feet as though something held them to the ground.

In offering presents as an ambassador, his appearance was sedate.

At a private audience, he wore a pleased look.

He would not eat meat that was clumsily cut, or served without its proper sauce. Although there might be an abundance of meat, he never let it exceed in quantity the vegetable food. In wine alone he laid down for himself no particular limit, but he never reached the stage of intoxication. He took ginger at every meal. He did not eat much. When eating, he did not converse; when in bed, he did not speak. Even though he had nothing but coarse rice and vegetable soup, he would always reverently offer some to the ancestral spirits.

He would not sit on a mat [1] that was placed awry.

On one occasion, Chi K'ang Tzŭ having sent him some medicine, he bowed as he received it,

[1] The Chinese of that date dispensed with chairs, as the Japanese have done up to the present time.

saying : Not being familiar with this drug, I would not venture to try it.

His stables having been burnt down, the Master on his return from the Court said : Has any one been hurt ?—He did not ask about the horses.[1]

If the Prince sent him a present of cooked meat, he would sit down to taste it on a properly placed mat.   If the Prince sent him a present of raw meat, he would have it cooked and offer it in sacrifice.   If the Prince sent him a live animal, he would keep it alive.

When the Prince summoned him to his presence, he would go on foot without waiting for his carriage.

If any of his friends died who was without a home or relations, he would say : I will see to the funeral.

In bed, he did not lie like a corpse.   In his home life, his manner was not too formal.

At the sight of a person in mourning, though it might be an intimate acquaintance, he would always look grave.   On meeting an official in uniform, or a blind man, however ragged, he would always show him some mark of respect.

[1] The point is, that in his solicitude for others Confucius never thought of his own loss, not that he was indifferent to the suffering of animals.

When a rich banquet was set before him, he would show his appreciation in his looks, and rise to return thanks.

He would change countenance at a thunder-clap or a sudden squall of wind.

When in his carriage, he would not look behind him, talk rapidly, or point with his finger.[1]

Duke Ling of Wei asked Confucius about the disposition of troops in warfare. Confucius answered : I know something about the arts of peace,[2] but I have never studied the art of war. And on the morrow he departed. But when he came to the State of Ch'ên, he was cut off from supplies,[3] and his followers were so enfeebled that they could hardly stand. Tzŭ Lu indignantly sought the Master's presence, saying : Is it for the princely man to feel the pinch of privation ?— The Master replied : Assuredly privation may

[1] Some of the minute details given above cannot but strike us as rather ridiculous. Two points, however, must be borne in mind : (1) that the customs and ceremonial belonging to any one age or country will always at first sight appear strange and laughable to the men of any other age and country ; (2) that Confucius himself cannot be held responsible for the excessive zeal which prompted admiring disciples to portray his personal habits with such embarrassing fidelity. How many philosophers would come equally well through such an ordeal ?

[2] Literally, " dish and platter business," i.e. things pertaining to sacrificial worship.

[3] By order of the Duke.

come his way, but it is only the baser type of
man who under it grows demoralised and reckless.

Mien, a blind musician,[1] having called on
Confucius, the Master said to him when he came
to a flight of steps : " Here are the steps " ;
and when he came to the mat which was spread
for him : " Here is your mat." When all the
visitors were seated, the Master told him who
they were, saying : So-and-so is sitting here,
so-and-so is sitting there. After Mien had gone,
Tzŭ Chang asked, saying : Is it the proper thing
to speak thus to a musician ?—The Master replied :
Assuredly it is right to give this help to a blind
man.

The people of Ch'i sent a band of singing-girls
as a present to the Duke of Lu, and Chi Huan Tzŭ
accepted the gift. For three days after that no
Court was held, and Confucius departed.[2]

---

[1] Blind men and musicians were almost convertible terms
in ancient China : that is to say, all musicians were blind,
and the majority of blind men took to music for a profession.

[2] The famous episode here briefly related was the turning-
point of the sage's career. Through the weakness of his
prince and the jealousy of the rival minister Chi Huan Tzŭ,
he was suddenly dislodged from the pinnacle of his fame and
condemned to thirteen years of homeless wandering.

CONFUCIUS AS SEEN BY OTHERS

Tzŭ Ch'in asked Tzŭ Kung, saying : Whenever our Master comes to any new country, he is sure to find out all about its method of government. Does he seek this information himself, or is it voluntarily proffered ?—Tzŭ Kung replied : Our Master gains his information because he is so genial and good, so full of deference, modesty and regard for others. In seeking information, how differently does he behave from ordinary men !

The Master having gone up into the Grand Temple, asked questions about everything. Some one remarked : Who says that the son of the citizen of Tsou has any knowledge of ceremonial observances ? He comes to the Temple and asks about everything he sees.—Hearing the remark, the Master said : This in itself is a ceremonial observance.

The prefect of the frontier in the town of I ¹ asked to be introduced to Confucius, saying : I

¹ This was on the borders of the Wei State, whither Confucius, with a small band of disciples, was retiring, heavy of heart, after his discomfiture in Lu.

have never failed to obtain an audience of any
sage who has visited these parts.—He was
thereupon introduced by the Master's followers,
and on coming out he said : My sons, why grieve
at your Master's fall from power? The Empire has
long been lying in evil ways, but now God is going
to make Confucius his herald to rouse the land.[1]

The Master said : Shên, a single principle runs
through all my teaching.[2]—Tsêng Tzŭ answered,
Yes.—When the Master had gone out, the disciples asked, saying : What principle does he
mean ?—Tsêng Tzŭ said : Our Master's teaching
simply amounts to this : loyalty to oneself and
charity to one's neighbour.[3]

---

[1] Literally, "is going to use him as a bell with a wooden
clapper"—this being the instrument used in making announce-
ments or to call the people together. The friendly prefect's
prophecy was to be fulfilled more wonderfully than ever he
could have imagined. Never, perhaps, in the history of the
human race has one man exerted such an enormous influence
for good on after generations.

[2] Legge's rendering, " My doctrine is that of an all-per-
vading unity," is quite untenable, and no other translator has
followed him here. The logic of the passage obviously requires the meaning given above.

[3] This saying should be compared with those on pp. 91
and 69. It is generally acclaimed as the best epitome of
Confucian teaching, yet it was reserved for Mr. Ku Hung-ming,
a Chinaman, to give the first correct translation of it in English.
The two important words are *chung* and *shu*, " conscientiousness " and " charity," for which see notes on pp. 58 and 69.
Legge's version, " To be true to the principles of our nature and
the benevolent exercise of them to others," though ponderous,
would seem to have hit the true meaning, had he not spoilt

Yen Yüan heaved a deep sigh and said : The more I look at our Master's teaching, the higher it seems. The more I test it, the more reliable it appears. I am gazing at it in front of me, when lo ! it is suddenly behind me. Our Master knows how to draw men after him by regular steps. He broadens our outlook by means of polite learning, and restrains our impulses by means of inward self-control. Even if I wished to stop, I could not do so ; yet after I have exhausted all my efforts in pursuit of the goal, there still remains something inaccessible rising up beyond ; and though I would fain make towards it, I cannot find the way.

Tzŭ Lu once passed the night in Shih-mên, where the gate-keeper said to him : Where do you come from ?—Tzŭ Lu replied : From the school of Confucius.—Oh, is he not the man, said the other, who is trying to do what he knows to be impossible ? [1]

it by a note to the effect that *shu* is " duty-doing on the principle of reciprocity." It has nothing on earth to do with reciprocity, being in fact that disinterested love of one's neighbour which was preached five hundred years later in Palestine. The other precept, embodied in the word *chung*, is exactly Shakespeare's " To thine own self be true "—a noble moral conception for which, obscured as it has been by bungling translators, Confucius has never yet received full credit.

[1] The age in which Confucius lived was so given over to the forces of disorder, militarism and intrigue, and the chances of a moral reformer were regarded as so hopeless, that it was

Ch'ên K'ang asked Po Yü,[1] saying : Have you ever received any secret teaching from your father ?—He replied : No. But once, when I was passing hurriedly through our hall, I met my father standing alone, and he said : Have you studied the Odes ?—I replied, Not yet.—He said : If you do not study the Odes, you will have no conversation.—Thereupon I withdrew and studied the Odes. Another day I met him again standing alone as I hastened through the hall, and he said : Have you studied the Book of Rites ?[2]—I replied : Not yet.—He said : If you do not study the Book of Rites, you will have no stability of character.—I withdrew and studied the Book of Rites. These are the two pieces of instruction I have received.—Ch'ên K'ang went away rejoicing and said : I asked about one thing and have learned three—some-

a common thing for men of principle to retire from public affairs altogether, and either lead the sequestered life of a hermit or take to some mean employment for a living. The gate-keeper here is said to have been one of this class. Confucius, however, was made of sterner stuff, and it may be claimed that he did ultimately, through sheer force of character, succeed in achieving the " impossible."

[1] The " style " or familiar name of K'ung Li, the only son of Confucius.

[2] Li here is obviously the name of a book, and not " the rules of propriety " or even " the arts," as Legge and Mr. Ku Hung-ming respectively take it. At the same time, we must be careful not to identify it with the now existing Li Chi or Book of Rites, which did not take shape until a much later period.

thing about the Odes, something about the Rites, and also that the higher type of man has no secrets even with his own son.

Yang Huo wished to have an interview with Confucius, but Confucius would not go to see him. He therefore sent Confucius a sucking-pig as a present.[1] Confucius, however, chose a time when the other was out, to go and pay his respects. But he happened to fall in with him on the road. Thereupon Yang Huo addressed Confucius, saying: Come with me. I have something to say to you. Can he be called truly benevolent, who hugs his jewel to his bosom and allows his country to drift into confusion?—He cannot, was the reply.—Can he be called truly wise, who wishes to engage in public affairs, yet loses several opportunities of doing so?—He cannot.—Well, rejoined Yang Huo, the days and months are fleeting by, and the years will not wait for us.—True, replied Confucius; I will presently take office.[2]

[1] Because etiquette would require an acknowledgment of the gift at the donor's house.

[2] This episode is probably to be referred to the year 502 B.C., when Yang Huo, the nominal subordinate of Chi Huan Tzŭ (himself of usurping tendencies, see Introduction, p. 15), was in open rebellion and seemed likely to become master of the whole state of Lu. He was anxious to enlist the prestige of a man like Confucius on his side, but the latter steadily refused to countenance his schemes. In the following year, Yang Huo was ejected from the state, and gratitude impelled the Duke to offer a governorship to Confucius.

The eccentric Chieh Yü [1] of the Ch'u State passed Confucius' carriage, singing : O phœnix ! O phœnix ! How has thy virtue fallen ! The past need no longer be a subject of reproof, but against the future it is still possible to provide. Desist, desist ! Great is the danger of those who now engage in government.—Confucius alighted, wishing to speak with him, but Chieh Yü hastened rapidly away, and he was unable to get speech of him.

Ch'ang Chü and Chieh Ni [2] were working together in the fields when Confucius passed by and sent Tzŭ Lu to ascertain from them the whereabouts of the ford. Ch'ang Chü asked : Who is that man holding the reins ?—That is Confucius, replied Tzŭ Lu.—Is it Confucius of the Lu State ?—Yes.—Then surely *he* is the man to know where the ford is.[3]—Tzŭ Lu then questioned Chieh Ni. Chieh Ni said : Who are you, Sir ?—I am Chung Yu.—Are you a disciple of Confucius of the Lu State ?—He replied : I am.— The whole Empire, said Chieh Ni, is rushing headlong to destruction, and who is there that will reform it ? As for you, instead of following a

---

[1] Apparently a Taoist, who pinned his faith to Lao Tzŭ's newly enunciated doctrine of inaction.

[2] Also Taoist recluses.

[3] This is said to be a sneer at the restlessness which kept Confucius wandering all over the country, so that no place could be unfamiliar to him.

man who withdraws from prince after prince in succession, would it not be better to follow a man who has withdrawn from the world altogether ?—And he went on hoeing without a pause. Tzŭ Lu went back and reported these remarks, whereupon the Master looked surprised and said : We cannot join the company of birds and beasts. If I am not to associate with these men of the ruling class, with whom am I to associate ? [1] If right principles prevailed in the Empire, then indeed there would be no need for me to reform it.

Shu-sun Wu-shu,[2] speaking to the ministers at Court, said : Tzŭ Kung is a greater sage than Confucius.—Tzŭ-fu Ching-po [3] repeated this to Tzŭ Kung, who said : Let me use the simile of a house surrounded by a wall. My wall rises only to the height of a man's shoulders, so that any one can look over and see the excellence of

[1] The idea is, " Every man to his own trade. Why should I not then busy myself with government—the subject to which I have devoted my life ? " I do not agree with Legge that the compiler of this chapter could not have been a disciple of the sage. Confucius successfully refutes the *laisser-faire* argument of the hermit, who would dissuade him from reform on the strange and unsatisfactory ground that the world's affairs were in a thoroughly bad state. To any one but a Taoist it would be evident that this was the very time for reform.

[2] A leading member of one of the three great families in the Lu State.

[3] A high official.

the building within. But my Master's wall is
many fathoms in height, so that one who fails
to find the gate of entry cannot see the beauties
of the temple nor the rich apparel of the officiating
priests. It may be that only a few will succeed
in finding the gate. Need we, then, be surprised
at His Excellency's remark ?

Shu-sun Wu-shu was disparaging Confucius.
Tzŭ Kung said : It is no good. Confucius is
proof against detraction. The wisdom of other
men is like hills and mountain-peaks, which
however high can still be scaled. But Confucius
is like the sun or the moon, which can never
be reached by the foot of man. A man may
want to cut himself off from their light, but
what harm will that do to the sun or the moon ?
It only shows very plainly that he has no notion
of the measurement of capacity.

SAYINGS OF THE DISCIPLES

Yu Tzŭ said : It is seldom that good sons and brothers are given to insubordinate conduct. That those who dislike insubordinate conduct should be ready to foment sedition, is something absolutely unknown. The wise man attends to the root ; for if this be properly set, virtue will spring from it. And what is the root of all goodness but filial piety and fraternal love ?

Tsêng Tzŭ said : There are three points on which I daily examine myself :—Have I been conscientious in working for others ? Have I been truthful in my intercourse with my friends ? Have I practised what I preach ?

Tzŭ Hsia said : The man who can appreciate moral worth and disengage his mind from sensual passion ; who can put forth his utmost strength to serve his parents, and lay down his life to serve his prince ; who speaks sincerely in his intercourse with friends :—such a man, though the world may call him untaught, has in my opinion received the best and highest education.

Tzŭ Kung said : What do you say of the poor man who refuses to flatter, and of the rich man

who is free from pride ?—They are well enough,
replied the Master ; but better still is the poor
man who is cheerful, and the rich man who
cherishes the inner principle of harmony and
self-control.—Tzŭ Kung said : One must " cut
and then carve, chisel and then polish," as the
Odes have it. Does not this passage illustrate
what you say ?—The Master exclaimed : Here
is somebody at last with whom I can really discuss
the Odes. Refer him to any old verse, and he
will see its application.[1]

Tzŭ Hsia asked, saying : What is the meaning
of the passage :
" What dimples in her witching smile !
What lovely eyes, clear white and black !
Simplicity sets off her ornaments " ?
The Master replied : You must have a plain
background before you can lay on the colours.—
Rules of ceremony then require a background ?—
Ah ! exclaimed the Master, Shang always seizes
my drift. Here at any rate is some one with
whom I can discuss the Odes.[2]

[1] Tzŭ Kung, who had passed from poverty to affluence,
wished to draw attention to his own freedom from the vices
characteristic of each state, but his Master recommends the
pursuit of virtue in a more positive form. The quotation from
the Odes merely enforces the necessity of unceasing labour
in the matter of self-improvement. Confucius was always
delighted with an apt illustration from his favourite book.

[2] The Chinese of the above is as usual extremely concise.
For several turns of phrase I am indebted to Mr. Jennings's
translation.

Tzǔ Yu said: Too much fault-finding with princes entails disgrace; with friends, it brings estrangement.

The Master wanted to employ Ch'i-tiao K'ai in the business of government, but the latter said: No, I cannot yet sufficiently trust myself.—The Master was pleased with the reply.

Once when Yen Yüan and Chi Lu were standing by, the Master said: Come, tell me, each of you, the wish of your hearts.—Tzǔ Lu said: I should like to have carriages and horses and fine fur garments, and share them with my friends; nor would I mind if they were worn out in this way.—Yen Yüan said: My wish is to make no parade of goodness and no display of toilsome service rendered.[1]—Tzǔ Lu then said: I should like, Sir, to hear your own wishes. The Master said: To comfort the aged, to win the confidence of my friends, to love and cherish the young.

The Master said: Yung might well be made a prince.[2] Chung Kung asked a question about Tzǔ-sang Po-tzǔ. The Master replied: He is a good man on the whole, though easy-going.—Chung Kung rejoined: Is it not excusable for a man who is strict in his own habits to be easy-going in dealing with the people under him?

[1] Literally, "display toil." The meaning seems to be that of the Tacitean phrase "exprobrare beneficia."
[2] Literally, "one who faces south"—the customary position for royalty enthroned.

But if he becomes easy-going in his own habits as well as in his practice abroad, this is surely too much of a good thing.—The Master said : Yung's words are true.

Jan Yu asked : Is our Master for or against the Prince of Wei ? [1]—Oh, said Tzŭ Kung, I will ask him that.—He went in and said : What sort of men were Po I and Shu Ch'i ? [2]—They were two ancient worthies, was the reply.—Did they ever repine ? he asked.—They made perfect virtue their aim, and they attained it. Why then should they repine ?—Tzŭ Kung went out again and said : Our Master is not for the Prince.

Tsêng Tzŭ said : Ability asking instruction of incompetence, abundance sitting at the feet of insufficiency, a man of every virtue who thought he had none, solid in character yet making himself out a cypher, trespassed against but never retaliating—such was the humble state of mind in which my late friend [3] spent his life.

Tsêng Tzŭ said : If a man can safely be entrusted with the care of a young orphan prince, or with the government of a large province, and if the approach of a great emergency cannot shake his resolution, is he not a man of the

[1] The reigning duke, who had succeeded his grandfather and was now opposing his father's attempts to return from exile and secure the throne.   See p. 43.

[2] See note on p. 74.

[3] The disciple Yen Hui.

princely type? Of the princely type he is
indeed!

The authorities of Lu were proposing to re-
construct the Long Treasury. Min Tzŭ-ch'ien
said: Why not restore it, rather, in the ancient
style? Why is it necessary to renovate it altogether?—The Master said: This man is no
talker, but when he does speak, he speaks to the
purpose.

Ssŭ-ma Niu lamenting said: All other men
have brothers; I alone have none.—Tzŭ Hsia
said to him: I have heard it said that life and
death are divine dispensations, that wealth and
rank depend on the will of God. The higher
type of man is unfailingly attentive to his own
conduct, and shows respect and true courtesy to
others. Thus all within the four seas [1] are his
brethren. How then should he grieve at having
no brothers?

Chi Tzŭ-ch'êng [2] said: The higher type of man
is possessed of solid qualities, and that is all.
What has he to do with the ornamental?—Tzŭ
Kung replied: I am sorry, Sir, to hear you say
such a thing about the higher type of man; for
a four-horse chariot cannot overtake the spoken
word. [3] The value of the ornament and the value

[1] Believed to constitute the boundaries of the habitable
earth, like Homer's Ocean-river. Hence the phrase is used
as a synonym for the Chinese Empire.
[2] A minister in the Wei State.   [3] A proverb.

of the substance are closely connected. Stripped of hair, the hide of a tiger or a leopard is very like the hide of a dog or a sheep.

Duke Ai asked Yu Jo, saying : It has been a year of famine. My exchequer is low. What am I to do ?—Yu Jo replied : Why not collect tithes ?—Why, said the Duke, with a tax of two-tenths I still have not enough. How am I to make one-tenth do ?—If the people have plenty, was the reply, how can the Prince alone be in want ? But if the people are in want, how can the Prince alone have plenty ?[1]

Tsêng Tzǔ said of the higher type of man that his culture tended to bring him into communion with friends, and his friendships tended to heighten his altruism.

The disciples of Tzǔ Hsia asked Tzǔ Chang about the principles which should govern friendship. Tzǔ Chang said : What is Tzǔ Hsia's opinion ?—They replied : Tzǔ Hsia says, Associate with those who come up to your standard ; reject all those who do not.—This, said Tzǔ Chang, is different from what I have been taught. The nobler sort of man honours the virtuous and wise, but he admits to his society all men without distinction. He admires the good, but he also pities the weaker brethren. Am I a man of great wisdom and goodness ?—then who is

[1] A rebuke to the Prince for his greed in a time of distress.

there among my fellow-men that I will not bear
with ?   Or am I neither wise nor good ?—then
other men will reject *me*.   How can one justify
this rejection of others ? [1]

Tzŭ Hsia said : The inferior type of man always
tries to gloss over his faults.

Tzŭ Hsia said : The wise man will gain the
confidence of the people before laying burdens
upon them ; otherwise, they will consider it
oppression.   He will gain the confidence of his
sovereign before censuring his actions ; otherwise,
the latter will consider it mere libel and abuse.

Tzŭ Hsia said : He who does not transgress
the larger principles of virtuous conduct may be
excused for disregarding the boundary line in
matters of smaller import.

Tzŭ Yu said : The followers and disciples of
Tzŭ Hsia are trained well enough in sprinkling
and sweeping the floor, in responding and answering questions, in entering and leaving a room.
But these are mere accessories.   Of fundamentals
they are totally ignorant.   How can this be
considered enough ?—Tzŭ Hsia, hearing of these
remarks, said : Ah ! Yen Yu is mistaken.   It

---

[1] Each pedagogue has seized only one side of the truth.
We need not reject any of our fellow-men, and yet show
discrimination in the choice of our associates. See the first
saying on p. 53, where Confucius, clearer-headed than his
disciples, puts the matter in a nutshell.

is not the way of the wise teacher to distinguish between subjects of first-class importance, which must be taught, and subjects of secondary importance, which may be neglected. He cultivates minds just as he would cultivate plants, each species requiring separate treatment. It cannot be the wise man's way to produce confusion and error. He only is inspired who teaches methodically, having a beginning and an end.

Tzŭ Hsia said : Let the official who has time to spare devote it to study ; let the student who has time to spare devote it to public affairs.

Tzŭ Yu said : The rites of mourning should not extend beyond the expression of heartfelt grief.

The chief of the Mêng family having appointed Yang Fu to be Criminal Judge, the latter went to Tsêng Tzŭ for advice. Tsêng Tzŭ said : Our rulers have lost their way, and the people have long been scattered and distracted. When you discover the facts of a crime, be not moved with joy but rather with pity and grief.

Tzŭ Kung said : The mistakes of a great and good man are like eclipses of the sun and moon : his failing is seen by all, and when he repairs it, all look up to him with awe.

The titles below are available in the Wisdom of the East Series. All are presented in heirloom-quality sewn, cloth bindings and are printed on acid-free paper. To order, if not available at your local bookseller, please phone toll-free 800-526-2778, or write: Charles E. Tuttle Company, Inc., P.O. Box 410, Rutland, VT 05702-0410

The Book of Mencius (abridged) translated from the Chinese by Lionel Giles (0-8048-1844-4)

A Confucian Notebook by Edward Herbert (0-8048-1793-6)

The Dhammapada: Sayings of Buddha translated from the Pali with notes by Narada Thera (0-8048-1845-2)

The Hymns of Zarathustra: Being a Translation of the Gathas with introduction and commentary by Jacques Duchesne-Guillemin (0-8048-1810-X)

Manifold Unity: The Ancient World's Perception of the Divine Pattern of Harmony and Compassion by Collum (0-8048-1811-8)

The Message of Islam: Being a Resume of the Teaching of the Qur-an: With Special References to the Spiritual and Moral Struggles of the Human Soul by A. Yusuf Ali (0-8048-1794-4)

The Perfection of Wisdom: The Career of the Predestined Buddhas: A Selection of Mahayana Scriptures translated from the Sanskrit by E.J. Thomas (0-8048-1795-2)

The Quest of Enlightenment: A Selection of the Buddhist Scriptures translated from the Sanskrit by E.J. Thomas (0-8048-1846-0)

The Road to Nirvana: A Selection of the Buddhist Scriptures translated from the Pali by E.J. Thomas (0-8048-1796-0)

The Sayings of Confucius: A New Translation of the Greater Part of the Confucian Analects by Lionel Giles (0-8048-1847-9)

The Sayings of Muhammad by Allama Sir Abdullah Al-Mamun Al-Suhrawardy (0-8048-1797-9)

The Song of the Lord: Bhagavadgita by E.J. Thomas (0-8048-1812-6)

The Spirit of Zen: A Way of Life, Work and Art in the Far East (2nd edition) by Alan W. Watts (0-8048-1798-7)

Tao Te Ching: The Book of the Way and Its Virtue by J.J.L. Duyvendak (0-8048-1813-4)